MAX KUEHNE

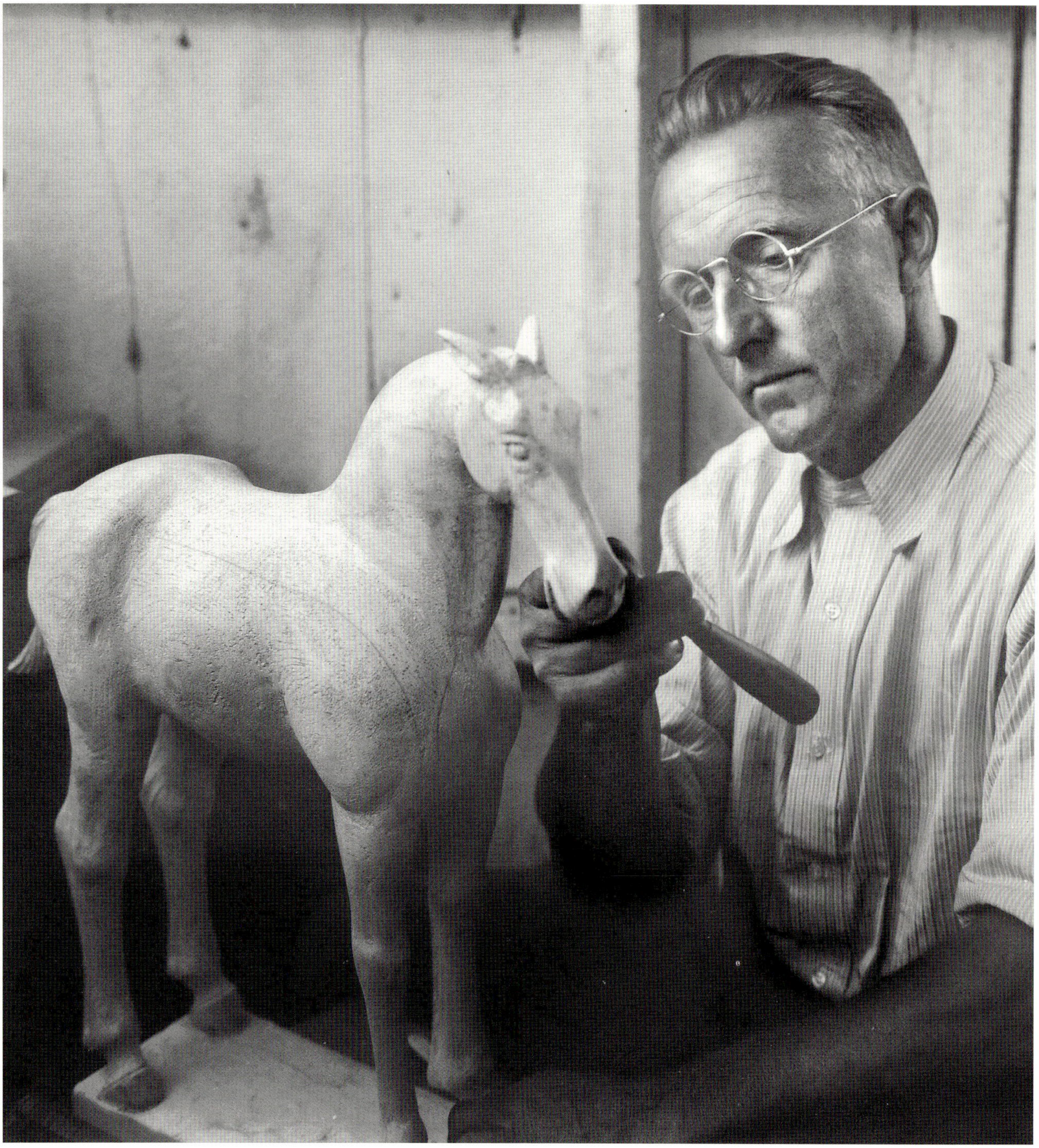

Max Kuehne

ARTIST AND CRAFTSMAN

HOLLIS TAGGART GALLERIES

48 East 73 Street, New York City 10021

IN MEMORIAM

Ronald G. Pisano, 1948–2000

A great gentleman and magnificent scholar

This catalogue has been published on the occasion of the exhibition "Max Kuehne: Artist and Craftsman," organized by Hollis Taggart Galleries and presented from 24 May to 23 June 2001.

The exhibition was curated by Vivian Bullaudy, Director of Hollis Taggart Galleries.

ISBN 0-9705723-3-6
Library of Congress Card Catalogue Number: 2001089519

Cover: Fire screen *(Deer and Leopard in Landscape)*, c. 1930s. Detail. Gessoed wood, watercolor, silver leaf, shellac, 35 × 25 × 11½ inches. Collection of Ann M. Beal
Frontispiece: Max Kuehne carving *(Horse)* in his studio, c. 1930. Photograph by Peter A. Juley & Son

Hollis Taggart Galleries
48 East 73 Street, New York, NY 10021
Tel 212 628 4000 Fax 212 717 4119
www.HollisTaggart.com

Publication Coordination: Kirsten Olds
Research: Kirsten Olds and Cynthia Seibels
Editing: Stephanie Salomon
Design: Russell Hassell, New York
Printing: Capital Offset, Concord, New Hampshire
Photography: All photographs by Helga Photo Studios with the exception of plate 7, Randl Bye; plates 26, 27, Christopher Erb; plates 16, 17, 19, 22, 35, Michael Lafferty Photography; plate 15, Gary J. Mamay; plates 1, 8, Jack Ramsdale Photography.

FOREWORD

The exhibition "Max Kuehne: Artist and Craftsman" presents a scholarly and wide-ranging overview of the multifaceted career of this artist. Recalling the Renaissance atelier concept of accomplishment in many areas of artistic expression, Max Kuehne was adept at woodworking, carving, gilding, sculpting, and printmaking, as well as painting—the medium for which he is primarily recognized today.

The idea for this exhibition, as with many of the others we have organized, evolved "organically." We needed a coffee table for one of our office spaces, and happened upon an exquisite example by Kuehne. Later, an incised panel, also by Kuehne, came our way. The delicacy and intricacy of its design and the unusual medium and technique used captured our imagination. After this second chance experience, the idea for an exhibition gathered momentum and eventually grew into its present form.

The exploration of the tension between function and artistry in Kuehne's work became a captivating topic, hence the duality embodied in the exhibition's title. The binary relationship Kuehne embraced became a means for him to synthesize a wealth of world cultures and techniques in his woodwork and paintings. Along with his colleague Charles Prendergast, Kuehne extended his artistic vision to include furniture and frame making.

The concept of showing three-dimensional objects in tandem with paintings and framed screens allowed us the creative freedom to conceive of different ways of organizing our gallery spaces. Planning the display of these artworks of varying size and medium challenged us and heightened our sensitivity to the unique elegance of each one. It also allowed us a rare entrée into the mind of the artist, whose loyal and steady patrons provided him with opportunities to design his artworks so that they would complement one another in a specific environment. The project afforded us the opportunity to focus on the interdisciplinary nature of Kuehne's work and the relationship of the artist's painting to his woodworking. Kuehne's love of working with wood prevailed throughout his career. Whether a sailboat mast, serving tray, folding screen, or intricately decorated chest, his production constantly reveals an intrinsic understanding of the texture and beauty of wood.

Max Kuehne spent a lifetime accumulating a knowledge of various techniques and crafts, including woodworking. This knowledge has been preserved by Richard Kuehne, the artist's son, who has continued in the tradition of his father and who has allowed us, through many in-depth conversations, a window onto the nature of his father's artistic endeavors. His generosity in lending us objects from his own collection as well as rare ephemera, such as photographs, sketches, and the artist's account books, has enabled us to present the true scope of Max Kuehne's achievements. We are grateful to Hal Kuehne, Richard's son, also a lender to the exhibition; he and his sister, Lindsay Turnquist, both continue to work in the gesso technique.

Professor Richard J. Boyle, a preeminent scholar of American art and former director of the Pennsylvania Academy of the Fine Arts, contributed a detailed essay on the artist, combining his extensive knowledge of the history of the decorative arts and his broad understanding of techniques and mediums. He is currently organizing a major traveling exhibition on the development of tempera painting in America. William B. Adair, director of the International Institute for Frame Study, a master frame maker, and curator of the traveling exhibition "The Frame in America," provided an illuminating essay on the processes involved in Kuehne's frame making and the importance of the artist's time spent in Spain.

Our sincerest gratitude for making this exhibition possible goes to Fred Baker, who offered us enthusiastic and unstinting support and assistance for this survey of Kuehne's work. The visionary Baker/Pisano Collection of art, from which a number of works by Kuehne in this exhibition were drawn, has been nurtured for over twenty years by Fred and his lifelong partner, Ronald G. Pisano, whose recent death we mourn and whose memory we honor. Ronald was a magnificent William Merritt Chase scholar and, above all, a great gentleman. The legacy they forged during their years of avid collecting and generous lending will be ensured through Fred's careful stewardship of the collection and his philanthropic goals for it.

Avis Berman, author of *Rebels on Eighth Street*, allowed us to come to know Juliana Force, the first director of the Whitney Museum of American Art and its forerunner, the Whitney Studio Club, and the impact of the patronage of both Force and the Whitney family on Max Kuehne. In addition, Ms. Berman loaned works that had been part of Juliana Force's collection to our exhibition. Ann S. Beal, a longstanding Kuehne patron, graciously offered her help and examples from her collection in order to preserve the historical importance of the artist's work and reaffirm interest in his career. We thank her and all the lenders who generously contributed to this exhibition. The support of another Kuehne patron, Archer M. Huntington, is manifested through the Hispanic Society of America, which he founded and which houses forty of the artist's paintings; at the Society, Curtis Burke, Curator of Paintings, and Diana Liddy, Rights and Reproduction Registrar, have shared our enthusiasm and aided us immensely in this project.

M. P. Naud and her colleagues at Hirschl & Adler Galleries have provided continual assistance and cooperation. We extend our appreciation to Larry Shar and his staff at Julius Lowy Frame and Restoring Company for their advice and expertise. To Franco Lissi, our heart-felt gratitude for his consummate mastery of the medium of conservation, and also for his innate understanding of the object itself. The seasoned staff at Hollis Taggart Galleries—Molly Eppard, Stacey Epstein, Debra Pesci, John Pils, and Glenn Spellman—reacted with creativity, accepting different roles in order to tackle this unique exhibition. In particular, recognition goes to Kirsten Olds and Cynthia Seibels for their dedicated work and original research, which yielded relevant primary sources used in the production of the catalogue, and also to Allyson Tasato Mellone for her invaluable assistance in the complex exhibition display. For their impeccable ability to bring to fruition the gallery's vision for the catalogue, we would like to thank Russell Hassell, our designer, Stephanie Salomon, our editor, and Jay Stewart of Capital Offset, our printer.

Hollis Taggart Vivian Bullaudy

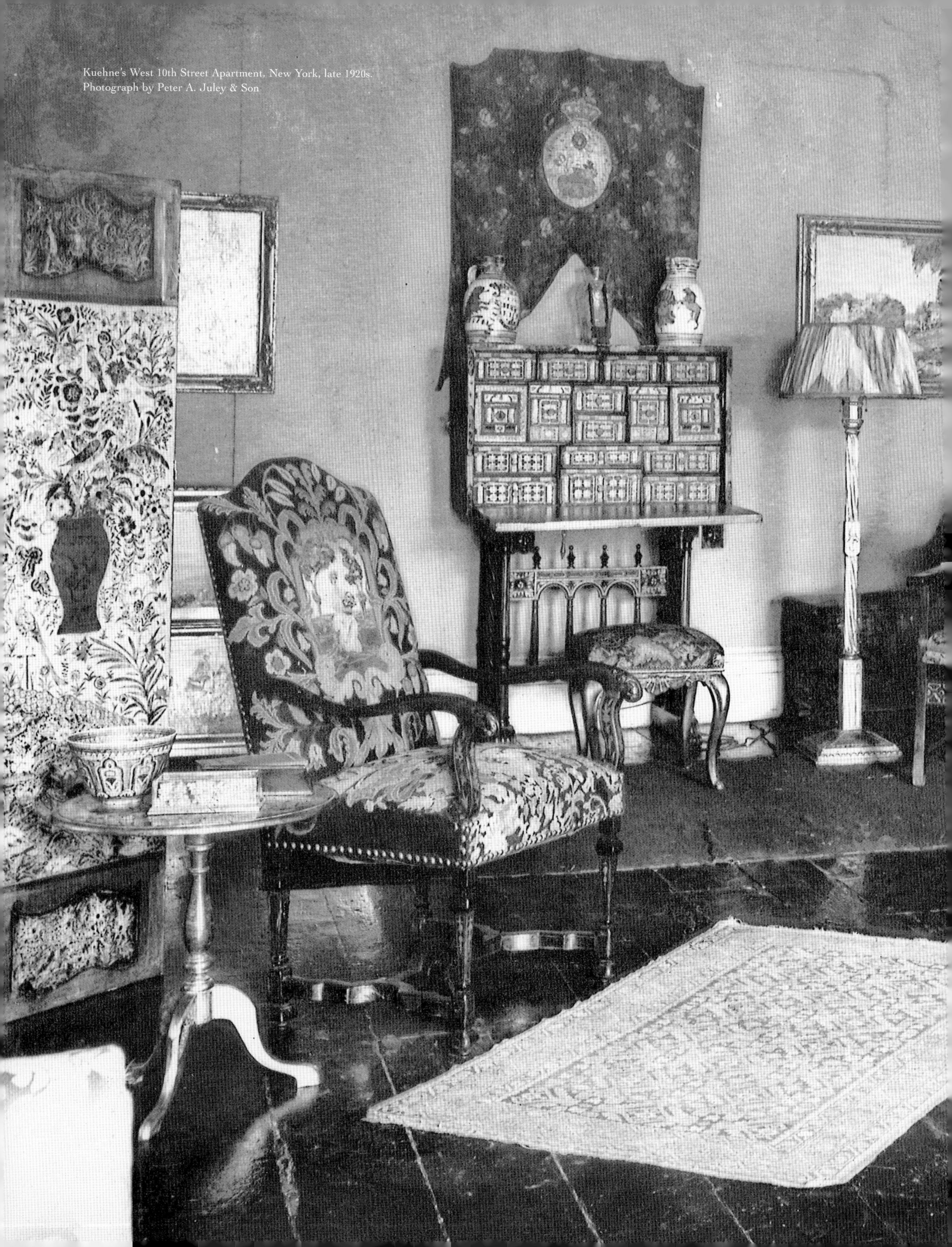

Kuehne's West 10th Street Apartment, New York, late 1920s.
Photograph by Peter A. Juley & Son

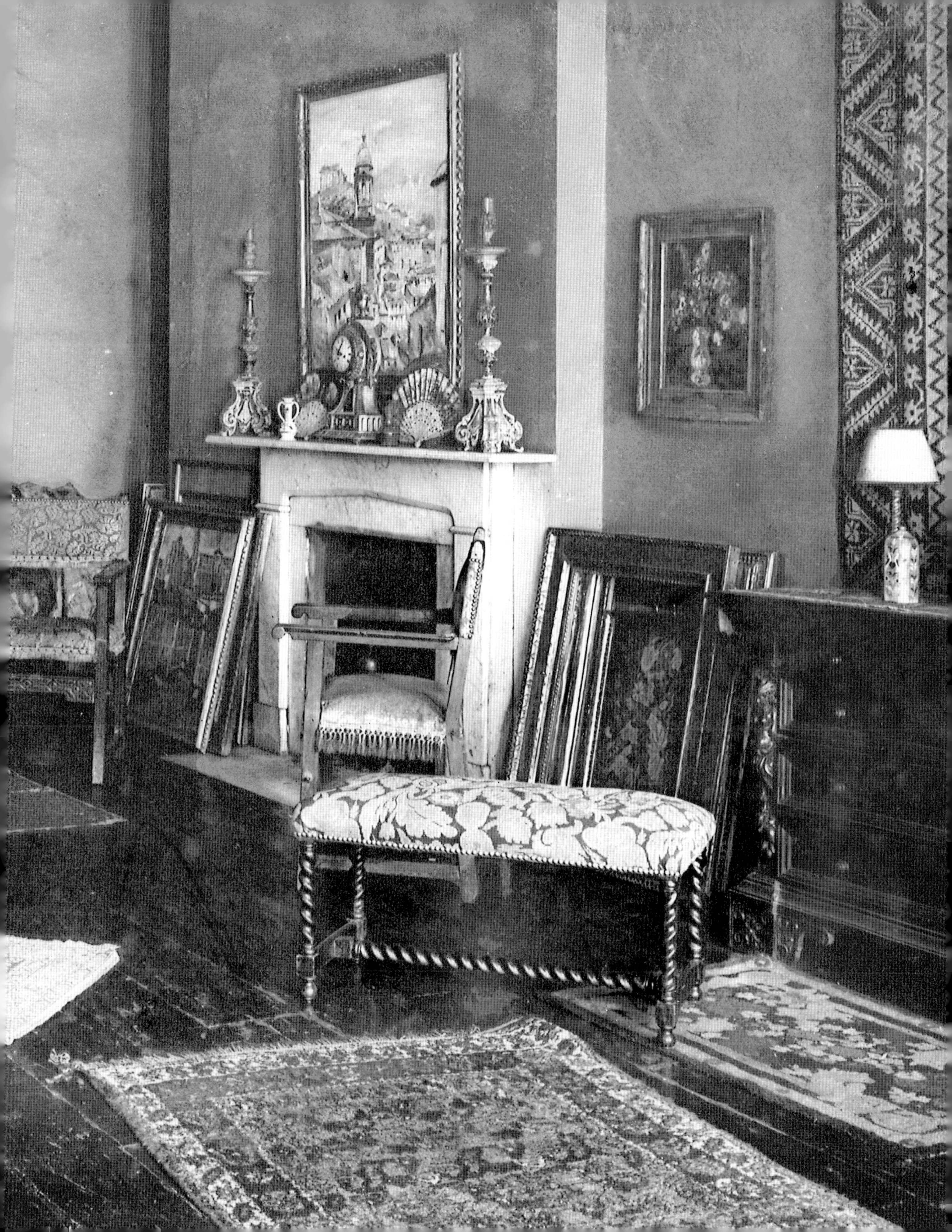

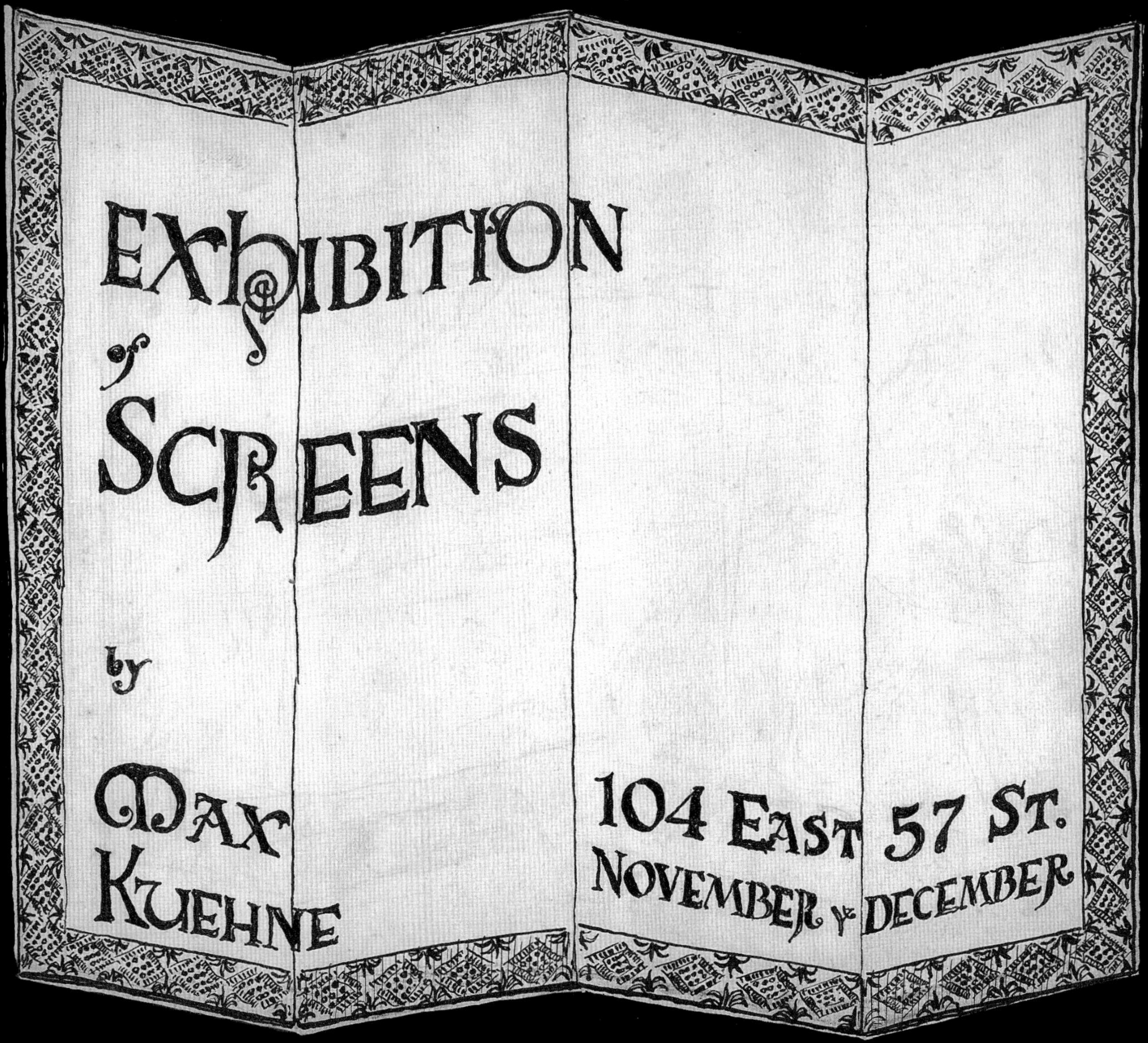

Advertisement designed by Max Kuehne for an exhibition of his screens, c. 1940s.

Family Reminiscences

RICHARD KUEHNE

WORK ROUTINE My father had his first studio apartment on Bank Street. In 1925 my parents moved to the second floor of an apartment at 29 West 10th Street. It was an area occupied by artists. I recall that Guy Pene Du Bois had an apartment across the street, and Luigi Lucioni lived near by. The sculptor William Zorach lived just across Sixth Avenue. The first artist-studio apartment building was on 10th Street—Stow Wengenroth had a studio there. I believe Eugene Speicher lived on Ninth Street as did John Johansen, a portrait painter of considerable note.

My father was always up and ready to work starting at 8:00 A.M., after the dog had been taken for a walk. Work on frame orders, screens, or tables continued through the morning. All fabricating and assembly work was done by hand in order to comply with the building codes.

Lunch was ready at noon. After lunch my father took the Scottie for a long walk. After returning home, the afternoon was spent the same way as the morning. My mother served tea at 4:00 P.M. This was the time that family friends generally dropped by for news and conversation. My father usually joined us for tea. Work in the shop continued until about 5:30 P.M. The dog had another walk just to obtain the evening newspaper. After dinner my father continued in his shop until the next day's work was laid out. Often, frames were assembled to allow the glue to set overnight. This routine was followed six days a week. On Sundays work proceeded in the morning; however, the afternoon was reserved for either museum or gallery visits.

In 1932 my family decided that the center of the art world had shifted to 57th Street. They were lucky to rent a second-floor apartment overlooking Park Avenue and 57th Street. Father installed one of his decorative screens in the window accompanied by a small placard that read: "Max Kuehne Screens." I am not sure, but I think the display resulted in several screen commissions. It was fortunate that I was always away at boarding school because the bedroom I might have occupied was used instead as my father's studio workshop. The arrangement continued when my family moved from 57th Street to a second-floor apartment at 25½ East 61st Street, just off Madison Avenue. The second bedroom was again used as a workshop. During this time I had completed college and served in the U. S. Naval Reserve (fig. 2).

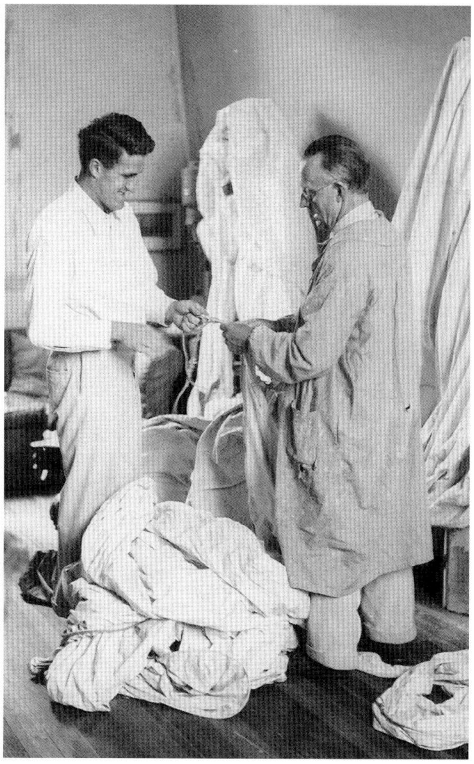

FIG 1 Max and Richard Kuehne examining a sail, Rockport, Massachusetts, c. 1939.

ROCKPORT, MASSACHUSETTS Like many of his fellow artists, my father spent his summers away from New York City. Ogden Pleissner and Luigi Lucioni summered in Vermont; Paul Manship, Gifford Beal, and Harrison Cady went to Cape Ann, Massachusetts. My father always set our date of departure from New York on Memorial Day. Even though my school was not quite over—I attended Friends Seminary on Rutherford Place—I was permitted to take special final exams in order to leave the city with my parents.

Summer routine differed from winter routine during the first ten or so summers spent in Rockport. Mornings were devoted to painting, sculpture in wood and gesso, and etchings. Afternoons were given over to beach life at Briar Neck. Since my father was one of the few artists who possessed a car, he picked up his fellow artists and drove them to the beach. I recall having to make the trips standing on the running board because the car was filled with passengers. The houses we rented during the summer were first in the area of Bearskin Neck in two different locations, and then the Eric Hudson house ("Hannah Jumper" house) on Mt. Pleasant Street. In 1937 the family bought their own house on Marmion Way. The house was remodeled from the designs of two local architects, which included a large second-floor studio workshop. The larger space enabled my father to continue his work in gesso as well as to paint.

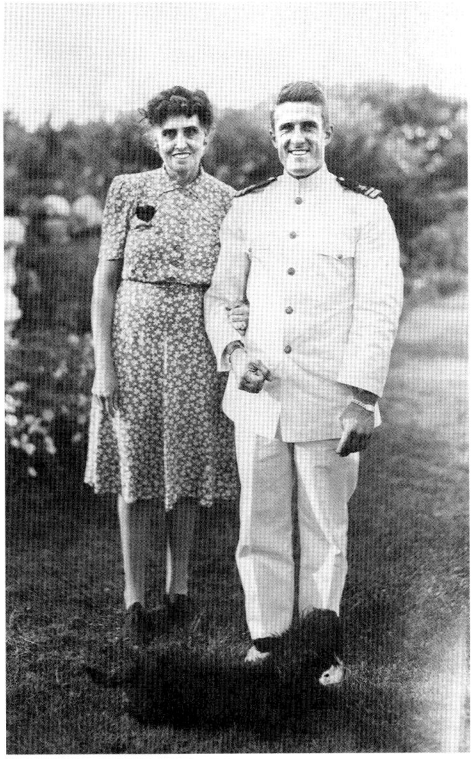

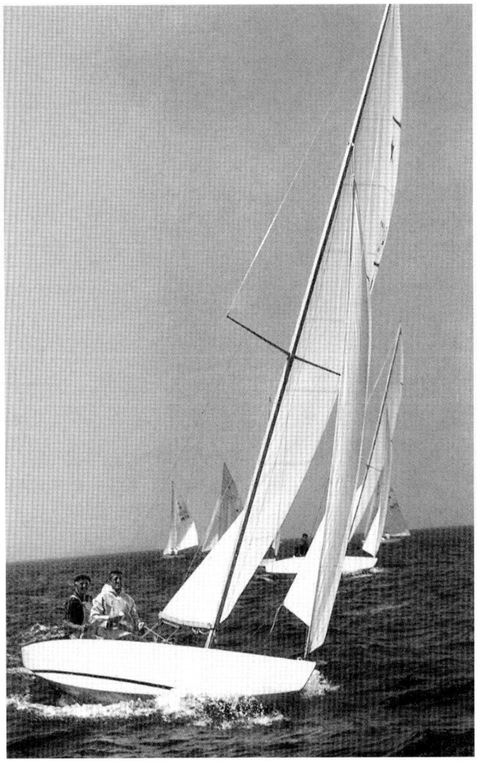

FIG 2 Margaret Kuehne, Richard, and "Muffin" in their garden in Rockport, Massachusetts, c. 1940.

FIG 3 Max and Richard Kuehne racing at the Sandy Bay Yacht Club, Rockport, Massachusetts c. 1930s.

In the early thirties my father bought a small sailboat, which we moored in Rockport Harbor. Soon afterward the Sandy Bay Yacht Club was built on "T" wharf, supplanting a coal-storage facility. Members of the Yacht Club purchased five "Star" racing-class boats, and so racing on weekends became a regular summertime occupation (fig. 3). My father's reputation as an artist was enhanced by his ability to glue wooden masts back together. "Star" masts, of what was then called "the new rig," were rather thin (32 feet tall) and made of laminated sitka spruce, a wood used in early aeroplanes. During a race a mast might snap in half at the spreader level. If a mast was broken during a Saturday afternoon race, it was brought to father's house for repair and regluing (fig. 1). The mast splice dried overnight, and was re-stepped Sunday morning; the boat was racing again that afternoon. Catastrophe and expensive repairs were averted.

Improvisation and quick results made with minimum effort were hallmarks of my father's philosophy, and extended to his well-being. In the early 1940s he fell off a high ladder in his studio at the house in Marmion Way. The accident resulted in two crushed vertebrae in the lower part of his spine. After spending three weeks in the Gloucester Hospital, he was discharged wearing a new type of cast made of fiberglass instead of the usual plaster. The cast came up from hip to armpit level. Most of our neighbors and friends thought my father's sailing was finished for the summer, if not forever. The first weekend home, my father was back racing while wearing the cast. Naturally he continued his artwork in his cast—which for him consisted of only a minor inconvenience.

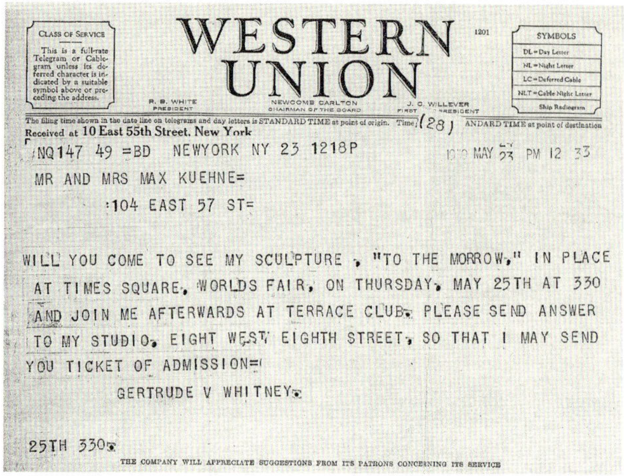

WESTERN UNION

CLASS OF SERVICE
This is a full-rate Telegram or Cablegram unless its deferred character is indicated by a suitable symbol above or preceding the address.

R. B. WHITE PRESIDENT — NEWCOMB CARLTON CHAIRMAN OF THE BOARD — J. C. WILLEVER FIRST VICE-PRESIDENT

1201

SYMBOLS
DL = Day Letter
NL = Night Letter
LC = Deferred Cable
NLT = Cable Night Letter
Ship Radiogram

The filing time shown in the date line on telegrams and day letters is STANDARD TIME at point of origin. Time (28) ANDARD TIME at point of destination

Received at 10 East 55th Street, New York

NQ147 49 =BD NEWYORK NY 23 1218P — 19 MAY 23 PM 12 33

MR AND MRS MAX KUEHNE=
:104 EAST 57 ST=

WILL YOU COME TO SEE MY SCULPTURE , "TO THE MORROW," IN PLACE AT TIMES SQUARE, WORLDS FAIR, ON THURSDAY, MAY 25TH AT 330 AND JOIN ME AFTERWARDS AT TERRACE CLUB. PLEASE SEND ANSWER TO MY STUDIO, EIGHT WEST EIGHTH STREET, SO THAT I MAY SEND YOU TICKET OF ADMISSION=
GERTRUDE V WHITNEY.

25TH 330.

THE COMPANY WILL APPRECIATE SUGGESTIONS FROM ITS PATRONS CONCERNING ITS SERVICE

FIG 4 Telegram sent by Gertrude Vanderbilt Whitney to Max Kuehne regarding her World's Fair sculpture, 1939.

My father enjoyed providing practical solutions for difficult problems. For example, for the 1939 World's Fair in New York, Mrs. Gertrude Whitney was commissioned to do a freestanding work of two figures on top of a twenty-four-foot-high, rainbow-shaped support set in the center of a circular pool. The sculpture, entitled *To the Morrow*, was cast in reinforced plaster. Mrs. Whitney, not satisfied with the result, asked my father what could be done to improve its appearance. Father recommended it be covered entirely with palladium leaf and volunteered to do the job. He once told me the only problem he had was keeping a distance from the union representative who wanted proof that he was a union member. Father solved that problem by staying up high in the scaffolding that surrounded the statue. The palladium was applied using an oil size for bonding with the plaster, which I am sure had to be covered with a varnish sealer before the size could be applied. The next problem was that Mrs. Whitney didn't like the color of the surrounding pool water. My father changed the color of the water by adding a gallon or so of bluing. In appreciation, Mrs. Whitney sent an invitation to Mother and Father by telegram to attend the installation ceremony for the statue (fig. 4). Mrs. Whitney showed her gratitude in other ways. During the Metropolitan Opera season in New York, she at times sent my mother tickets for her box seats, which were located just to the right center of the golden horseshoe. They were always delivered to our apartment via her maroon-colored Rolls Royce and chauffeur. I recall attending a matinee performance with my mother, the first time I had witnessed a performance from a box.

SOCIAL NOTES Part of the business life of an artist revolved around exhibiting one's work in pleasant surroundings. My mother had a keen interest in furniture and the decorative arts. She attended the exhibitions and sales of a number of auction houses in New York, acquiring at bargain prices fine chairs and pieces of decorative art that served to complement my father's work in gesso. The aim was to make the living room into an understated showroom. It was an education for me to walk down Madison Avenue with her and view the window displays of the many art dealers specializing in furniture, china, silver, textiles, and sculpture. I always enjoyed her comments on what was good and what was not.

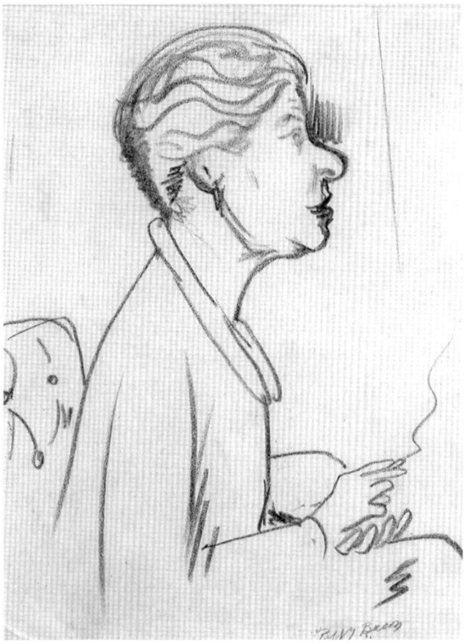

FIG 5 Peggy Bacon, *Portrait of Juliana Force*, 1931. Crayon on paper, 11½ × 8½ inches. Baker/Pisano Collection

Besides maintaining what I suppose amounted to an elegant salesroom, my mother entertained prospective clients and friends for dinner. For these occasions she usually engaged a cook and waitress to help her serve dinner. I recall preparations for eight in which the majolica dinner plates were laid out for service. My father, noticing that in some instances the colored borders of the plates were chipped, decided to improve their appearance by touching them up with oil paint. The result was not apparent until dinnertime when several of the guests found their napkins smudged with oil paint and their mouths ringed in oil.

One other footnote concerning my mother. In her account books, not only were expenditures and sales of furniture recorded, but also her investments in stocks. She had the facility of charming dour bankers and lawyers at parties into giving her tips on stocks and incipient mergers. For example, Thomas J. Watson, whom my mother met at a cocktail party for New York artists, advised her to invest in IBM stock. She followed his advice, which over the years proved to be profitable.

Other than Gifford Beal's annual Christmas party and Juliana Force's Christmas Day party in her top-floor apartment at the Whitney, there wasn't too much social activity in New York that I can recall (fig. 5). Social activities were much more frequent in Rockport. I can remember Antoinette Kraushaar, her brother

Buddy, and her father joining us at the beach in Briar Neck. Frank Rehn summered in Briar Neck. Leon Kroll and Paul Manship were in Lanesville, and Francis Taylor, director of The Metropolitan Museum of Art, summered in Annisquam and came to visit the family in Rockport. The art photographer Peter Juley made Rockport one of his summer stops. The family's best mode of entertainment was late afternoon gatherings of artists and summer visitors. The basic libation at these parties was "fish house punch," an innocuous brew that, when consumed in large quantities during the course of a hot summer evening, caused some of the family's more staid guests to lose their inhibitions. A jolly time was had by all.

The Beals also held a card party called "Michigan," for which you were given a bundle of matches. If you lost your matches, due perhaps to the luck of the draw, you were out of the game. Besides the card parties, the Beals had an annual Fourth of July party that featured small rockets shot out over the water in the backyard of their Bearskin Neck cottage.

My father, always interested in photography, purchased an 8mm Bell & Howell movie camera. With this he documented summer life in Rockport, emphasizing sailing. He also used it to film an amateur theatrical production entitled *Stone Fences* in which different characters were depicted by members of the Rockport art colony.

THE LATER YEARS After the death of my mother in the autumn of 1960, my father lived in his apartment in New York and his summer home in Rockport. He never varied his routine and was perhaps busier than ever. Charles Gracie, a friend of my father's and a dealer in antique Chinese wallpaper and furniture, had exhibited examples of my father's work, particularly large chests and coffee tables. During the autumn, winter, and spring months, my father spent weekends at my house in Rock Tavern, New York. He arrived every Saturday morning after picking up his car, accompanied by his Scottie and a large beef roast and bottle of wine, together with pieces of wood that required cutting to his measurements by the bandsaw I had installed in my shop. Sunday afternoon he returned to the city. In the event of a snowstorm that promised perhaps hazardous driving conditions, he could never be persuaded to extend his visit until the following day. He had to be at work on Monday morning and that was that.

It was during his later years that my father returned to painting. In the late 1940s, I believe, I had accompanied him to a retrospective exhibition of paintings by Pierre Bonnard. Father decided to apply Bonnard's technique and palette to create his own compositions. I believe he once told me that instead of concentrating on one painting he would work up four or more paintings at a time. Working on one or two paintings a day, he would then set them aside. Returning to each painting, he could more easily see what remained to be done. When after perhaps close scrutiny he could find nothing to add, the painting was judged and set aside as finished.

Later in his life my father came up to Rockport earlier and stayed later into the autumn. He had decided to stop sailing and racing in the "Star" class only to order a larger racing boat, the Etchells-22. He thought he could promote the boat both as a racing and sailing class for its builder and designer, Skip Etchells. Unfortunately this never came to pass. My father died in his sleep in his New York apartment on the night before he was to return to Rockport to lay a mooring in the harbor for what was to be his new boat.

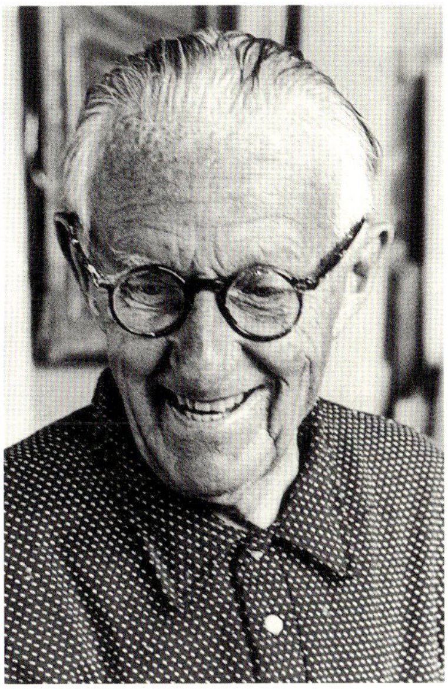

FIG 6 Max Kuhne, c. 1960s.

SUMMING UP The legacy of my father continues to play an important part in my life. For over fifty years I have worked in his medium: gesso and gilding. I now live in Rockport, a town in a larger community that includes him as part of the Cape Ann legacy in the arts. Every day I am reminded of his work in the design of a perhaps humble but visually important artifact—the weather vane atop the cupola of the Sandy Bay Yacht Club. This past year I was able to gild the weather vane in gold leaf, so that it gleams against the darkening evening sky. What better memorial could one have than that?

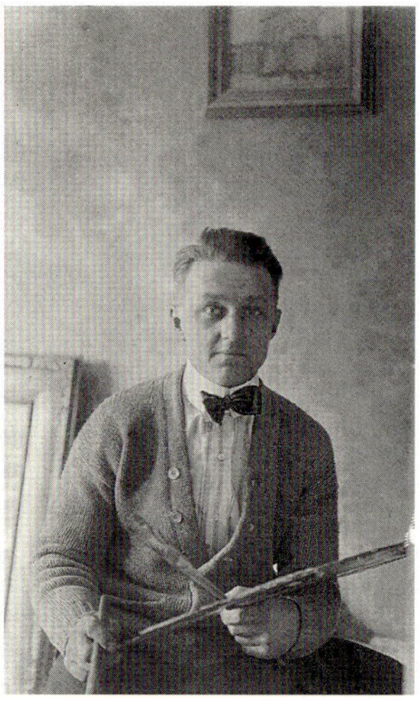

I am a carpenter, a designer, a painter, and a gilder.
—Max Kuehne to Ann Beal, late 1950s

Mr. Kuehne's gesso…In his own estimation…
stands on a par with his art as a landscape painter;
in no way does he consider it less worthy of his effort.[1]
—Horace Wesley Ott, 1926

Max Kuehne

ARTIST AND CRAFTSMAN

RICHARD J. BOYLE

Like many artists of his generation, Max Kuehne is something of a rediscovery. He was a landscape painter who also became known for his proficiency as a frame maker, as well as for his imaginative production of decorative furniture and carvings. Although his work in the latter disciplines helped him to survive, first as an emerging artist in the late teens and early twenties, then through the Great Depression of the 1930s, it was also work in which he had a genuine creative interest as well as enormous talent and consummate skill. In this study of Max Kuehne's oeuvre, strong emphasis is placed on his furniture and carvings and on his adaptation of the early Renaissance technique of incised and gilded gesso on wood, often including subtle variations of color. It comes at a time when distinctions among media are being erased and the line between the fine and the decorative arts has become blurred, a phenomenon to which Max Kuehne himself made a significant contribution.[2]

Born in Halle, Germany, in 1880, Max Kuehne immigrated with his family to New York in the 1890s, first to Flushing, then to Weehawken, New Jersey, at that time a rural area and a site from which John Marin would later paint watercolors of Manhattan, across the Hudson River. Kuehne worked at several jobs, including as a dental laboratory assistant and a printer's apprentice (both of which would have involved manual skill and a fair degree of precision). In 1907, however, he began his career as an artist by studying with William Merritt Chase (1849–1916) and Kenneth Hayes Miller (1876–1952) at the former's New York School of Art, a studio school where Robert Henri (1865–1929) also taught for a time before starting his own classes.

From Chase, Kuehne learned to use the high-keyed color of an Impressionist palette, a vigorous approach to the canvas, and virtuoso brushwork (Chase, like John Singer Sargent, was an artist blessed with "fast hands"). Miller taught a more structured approach to picture making—a more considered method of composition. He was a more intellectual artist than either Chase or Henri, and was also obsessed by the Italian Renaissance—its art and its crafts—an obsession that was probably beginning to take hold around the time Kuehne studied with him. Thus, it is possible that Kuehne might have been introduced to working with gesso as Miller's student. In addition, there was a revival of interest in traditional methods and materials at that time, of which the use of a gesso ground for painting was a part, and Modernists such as Alfred Maurer employed the brilliant white of this type of ground.

Following a stint as a student at the National Academy of Design in 1908, Max Kuehne joined Robert Henri's night school classes in 1909, the year Henri started his own school. Kuehne had the good fortune to study with three of the most outstanding teachers in America, but according to the artist's son, Richard, Henri probably had the most influence on his father.[3] Robert Henri was an exceedingly talented artist dedicated to capturing the spirit of modern life, as well as an extremely charismatic teacher who rejected the status quo represented by the more conservative National Academy of Design. He fostered and encouraged individuality, and believed deeply in the promise of an American art. His students were legion; among them, besides Kuehne, were George Bellows, Guy Pene Du Bois, Stuart Davis, Jo Nivison (later Mrs. Edward Hopper), and Rockwell Kent and Edward Hopper, both of whom became Kuehne's friends (Hopper would occasionally baby-sit Max Kuehne's son). In addition, Henri provided an entrée to the exciting part of the New York art world over which he presided, which included members of the group The Eight, such as Ernest Lawson and Maurice Prendergast. Kuehne traveled in Spain with Lawson; and Maurice Prendergast, along with his brother Charles, became lifelong friends.

New York was a dynamic place for a young artist to be during the first three decades of the twentieth century. It was the New York of Gertrude Vanderbilt Whitney (fig. 1). Gertrude (1875–1942) was the daughter of Cornelius Vanderbilt II, reported to be the richest man in America, and she was the great-granddaughter of Cornelius "Commodore" Vanderbilt, who founded the family fortune. She married Harry Payne Whitney in 1896. Although she was, in the words of Avis Berman, "daughter of one millionaire and married to another . . . she tired of her endless leisure and slowly sought a focus for her existence . . . she emerged as . . . a serious sculptor and one of

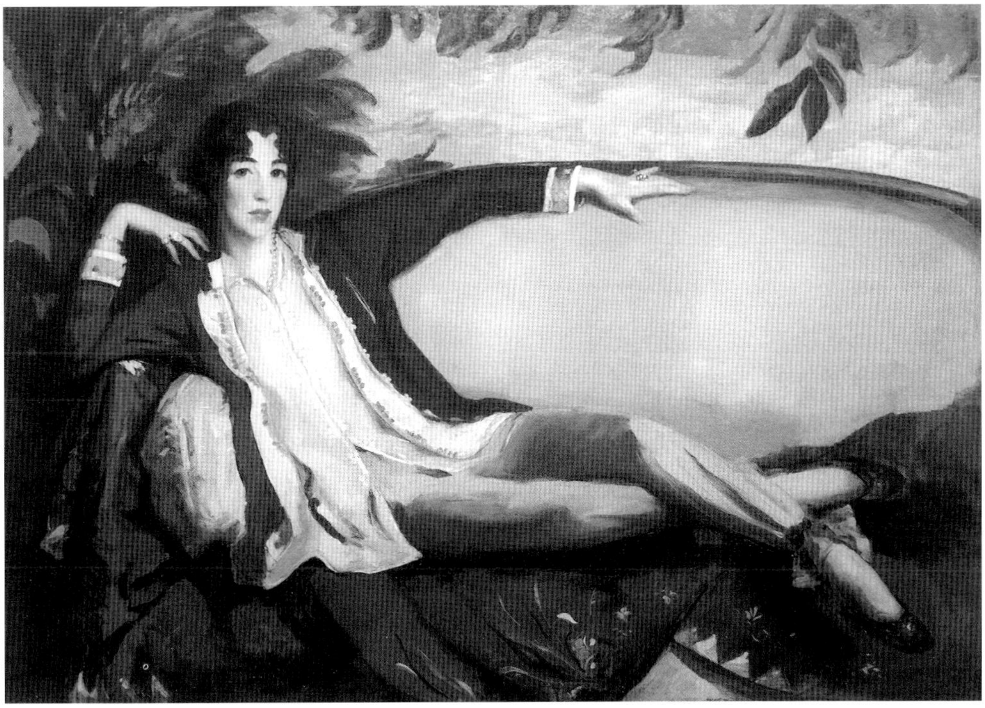

FIG 1 Robert Henri, *Gertrude Vanderbilt Whitney*, 1916. Oil on canvas, 50 × 72 inches. Gift of Flora Whitney Miller. © 1986 Whitney Museum of American Art, New York

the most important patrons in the history of American art." It was also the New York of Alfred Stieglitz who from his famous gallery, "291," located at 291 Fifth Avenue, tirelessly championed the work of John Marin, Max Weber, Arthur Dove, and other American Modernists. The city was exciting and it was cheap; Kuehne and his friends had a good time. There was Stanford White's Madison Square Garden (torn down in 1926), a Hispano-Moorish pleasure palace, considered as much a part of the city as the Battery or Central Park. There were the fashionable restaurants Delmonico's and Sherry's, located where, wrote Karl Baedeker in his celebrated guide, "above 47th and Fifth private residences form perhaps an imposing show of affluence and comfort [more] than any other street in the world."[4] Below 47th Street was Mouquin's and, especially, the Café Francis. The Francis, on 35th Street, was one of the most popular watering holes for New York's artists and writers and a gathering spot for Henri and his friends. Farther downtown, the National Academy of Design was housed on 23rd Street and farther still, Greenwich Village was well on its way to becoming New York's Left Bank and the bohemian capital of the country; it was where Max Kuehne would settle when he returned from Europe.

In 1910, following his formal training in art, Kuehne went abroad to continue his studies and to paint, and particularly to see the work of the Old Masters. "Father recognized the necessity of studying the works of the Old Masters as an adjunct to painting," wrote Richard Kuehne, "and over the years he spent considerable time in the major galleries of Europe."[5] On this particular trip—paid for by painting portraits along the way—during which the artist visited France, Belgium, Holland, and Germany, he made extensive notes on the paintings he saw in Holland. Although he later became interested in Neo-Impressionism and aspects of Post-Impressionism, his response to the more modernist movements was largely conservative and his painting continued to be variations on a combination of modified Realism and Post-Impressionism until late in his career when he came under the spell of Pierre Bonnard. It was on the German leg of this trip that he met his future wife, Margaret Gresser, whom he would marry in 1913.

In 1911, Kuehne returned to New York and in 1912 he spent his first summer in Gloucester on Cape Ann, drawn there, he said, "by seeing Childe Hassam's paintings of Gloucester Harbor."[6] In fact, one of his Gloucester Harbor scenes, *Motif #1,* was painted from the same vantage point on Banner Hill as Hassam's; John H. Twachtman and Willard Metcalf also painted the town's busy harbor from that site (fig. 2). To a landscape painter like Kuehne, a sense of place was important. Yet, he would not return to Cape Ann until 1918 and then intermittently thereafter. From about 1925 on, however, he spent his summers in Rockport, just a few miles from Gloucester. But before Rockport his strongest geographical influence, one where his sense of place was first challenged and inspired, was Spain.

The Kuehnes moved to Spain in 1914 where they lived principally in Granada, and later in Segovia. The move was to have a lasting impact on the artist. Not only did he produce paintings of great strength—of sharply delineated form and brilliance in color—he also developed his skills in wood carving and frame making by watching, as his son related, "Spanish craftsmen working in a long-standing tradition."[7] Kuehne lived there until 1917 and returned several times throughout the 1920s, as "one could enjoy the use of a house and servants for what it would cost to rent a cold water flat in New York," according to Richard Kuehne.[8] Spain was not only cheap, but possessed an extraordinarily rich culture and an artistic tradition that had resonated with artists at least since Manet introduced Spanish subject matter in the 1860s. For American painters, writes Elizabeth Boone, "Spain and Spanish art played an important, but under-recognized, role . . . between the years 1860 and 1920."[9] Two of Max Kuehne's

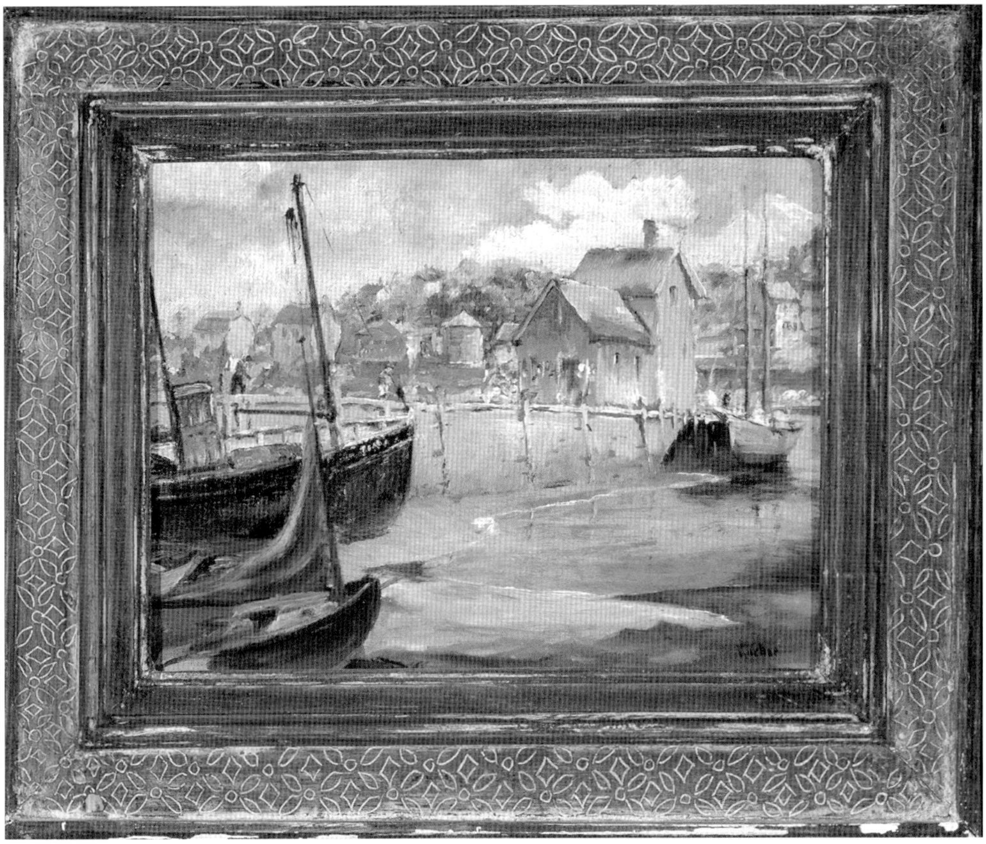

FIG 2 Max Kuehne, *Motif #1*, c. 1937. Oil on plywood, 12 × 16 inches, signed lower right: "Kuehne." Frame by Max Kuehne. Collection of Mr. Hal Kuehne

teachers, William Merritt Chase and Robert Henri, brought their students to Spain; Henri and many of his colleagues looked to Velázquez and Goya as models.

If Kuehne was in good company, he also chose a marvelous site. Granada is the home of the Alhambra, the best-preserved Islamic monument left in Spain, the present form of which dates from the fourteenth century. Built on a hill overlooking the town, it constitutes a remarkable ensemble of Islamic architecture and art, lush courtyard gardens, mosaics and colorful tiles, and elegant kufic calligraphy and exquisite woodwork. It was in fact the essence of Moorish Spain celebrated for centuries and popularized for Americans in Washington Irving's *Tales of the Alhambra*. Granada itself, with its picturesque streets, is also home to the largest still-inhabited Arab quarter in the West. It is not surprising that Max Kuehne developed an interest in decorative furniture, or that he painted some of his best landscapes there. "It was during this period," wrote his son, "that Father did most of his Spanish paintings [for example, *Spanish Town on Hillside*, pl. 28]; while learning to speak Spanish like a native, he accumulated a collection of paintings and sketches of Spain".[10] The Kuehnes also collected antique Spanish furniture and artifacts. In 1922, thirty-two of the artist's Spanish paintings were bought by the collector and Hispanophile Archer M. Huntington (c. 1871–1955) for the Hispanic Society of America, which he had founded in New York in 1904 (fig. 3).[11] "[T]o me also," wrote the collector and critic A. E. Gallatin in 1924, "Kuehne's pictures suggest the grandeur and grimness of the Spanish landscape . . . and her general austerity to a remarkable degree" (fig. 4).[12]

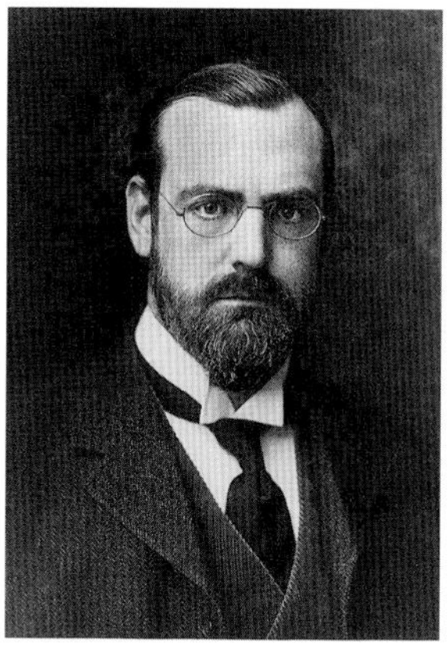

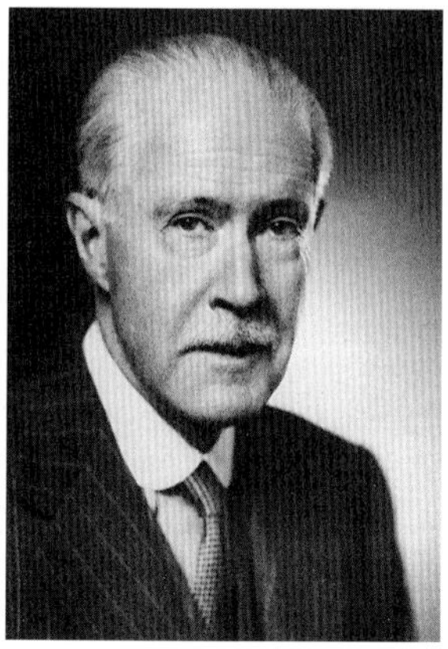

FIG 3 (left) Archer M. Huntington, c. 1900. Courtesy of the Hispanic Society of America

FIG 4 (right) Albert E. Gallatin, c. 1940s. Courtesy of University Archives, New York University. Photograph by Pach Brothers

It was during this period of trips to Spain in the 1920s that Max Kuehne's career began to hit its stride. "The first recollection that I have concerning my father as an artist dates from the time when I was about five years old. I remember him engaged in tacking canvas to a stretcher in. . . a house in Frickenhausen-am-Main, where he and my Mother were visiting. This was . . . a painting trip that had started in the Balearic Islands, continued to Lisbon and then to Granada, and . . . was to end in Paris before returning to New York."[13] A typical painting from this period is *Montmartre* (pl. 29), 1923, a view of the celebrated artists' quarter in Paris emphasizing, as Kuehne did in his Spanish paintings, the architectural qualities of the scene but with a placement and treatment of trees in the foreground reminiscent of paintings by Cézanne.

Returning to New York in 1917, Kuehne's Spanish and European landscapes were well received, and he exhibited them widely, especially during the 1920s. In 1917, he showed his work in one of the early exhibitions presented at the Whitney Studio Club (the forerunner of the Whitney Museum of American Art), which would become a major source of support for the artist. The exhibition featured contemporary landscapes and also included the work of Maurice Prendergast, Charles Demuth, Glenn O. Coleman, Augustus Vincent Tack, Paul Burlin, and the young Stuart Davis. The Whitney Studio Club, located on West Eighth Street, was sponsored by Gertrude Vanderbilt Whitney and administered by Juliana Force (1876–1948), who ran it in an informal manner; she not only organized exhibitions, but held sketching classes and provided a place for artists to congregate. The Kuehnes lived nearby. "In New York," wrote Richard Kuehne in "A Reminiscence," "we lived first on Bank Street . . . and then for many years on West Tenth Street."[14] Their neighbors in that vicinity were part of a lively community of artists that included the fascinating and stylish Realist Guy Pene Du Bois; Robert Henri's friend and an original member of The Eight, William Glackens; and the Modernist sculptor William Zorach. "I remember visiting Charles Prendergast in his studio on Fourteenth Street," notes Richard Kuehne. "The Hoppers came to visit as well as Dr. Albert Barnes of Philadelphia. . . ."[15] Barnes not only bought several of Kuehne's paintings, but he also commissioned three chests of drawers built and decorated by the artist, a craft inspired by Spanish artisans and one that developed from Kuehne's work with frames.

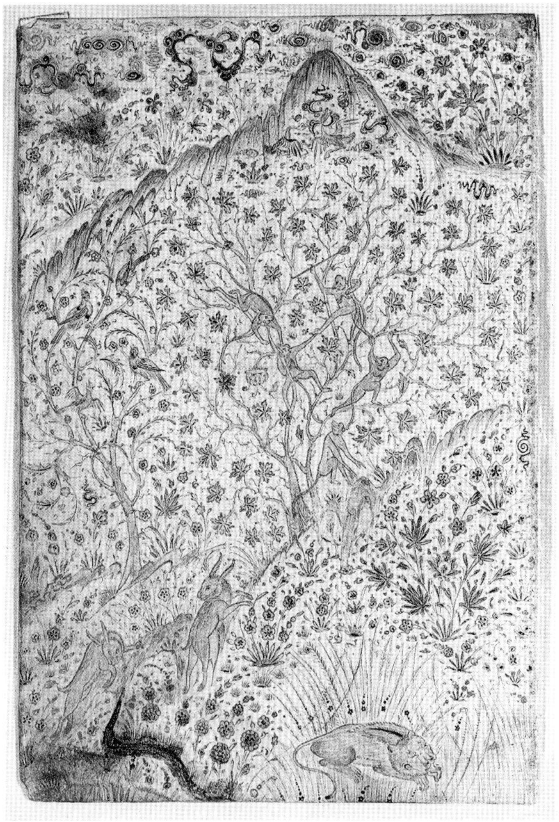

FIG 5 Unknown Persian artist, illuminated page, 16th century. Painted in gold and blue, 9⅜ × 6¼ inches. Courtesy of The Metropolitan Museum of Art, Purchase, Joseph Pulitzer Bequest, 1952

When he returned to New York in 1917, Kuehne began making his own frames, not only to save money but also to be able to obtain exactly the quality of frame he wanted. He became accomplished in this area and was soon supplying frames to fellow artists such as Gifford Beal, Randall Davey, William Glackens, Ernest Lawson, Edward Manigault, Charles Sheeler, Kenneth Hayes Miller, and Rockwell Kent. He even made frames for Maurice Prendergast on occasion. In addition, he supplied frames to such well-known New York art galleries as Daniel and Kraushaar, as well as to Knoedler and Durand-Ruel, and to the Whitney Studio Club. Also in 1917, he entered into a partnership with Rockwell Kent to produce a series of framed mirrors, which included images by Kent on reverse-painted glass panels mounted above the mirror portion.

From there it was but a short step to the decorated furniture and other objects, including folding screens, fire screens, beds, various chests, tables of all kinds, desks, serving trays, and incised panels; Kuehne also carved wooden sculptures, which he finished in silver or palladium leaf. The decorative motifs Kuehne used initially were an eclectic mix based on various cross-cultural sources—Spanish, French, Islamic, Coptic, Persian, Western medieval, Italian Renaissance, and Japanese (figs. 5, 6). In the 1930s his work was inspired primarily by Coptic motifs

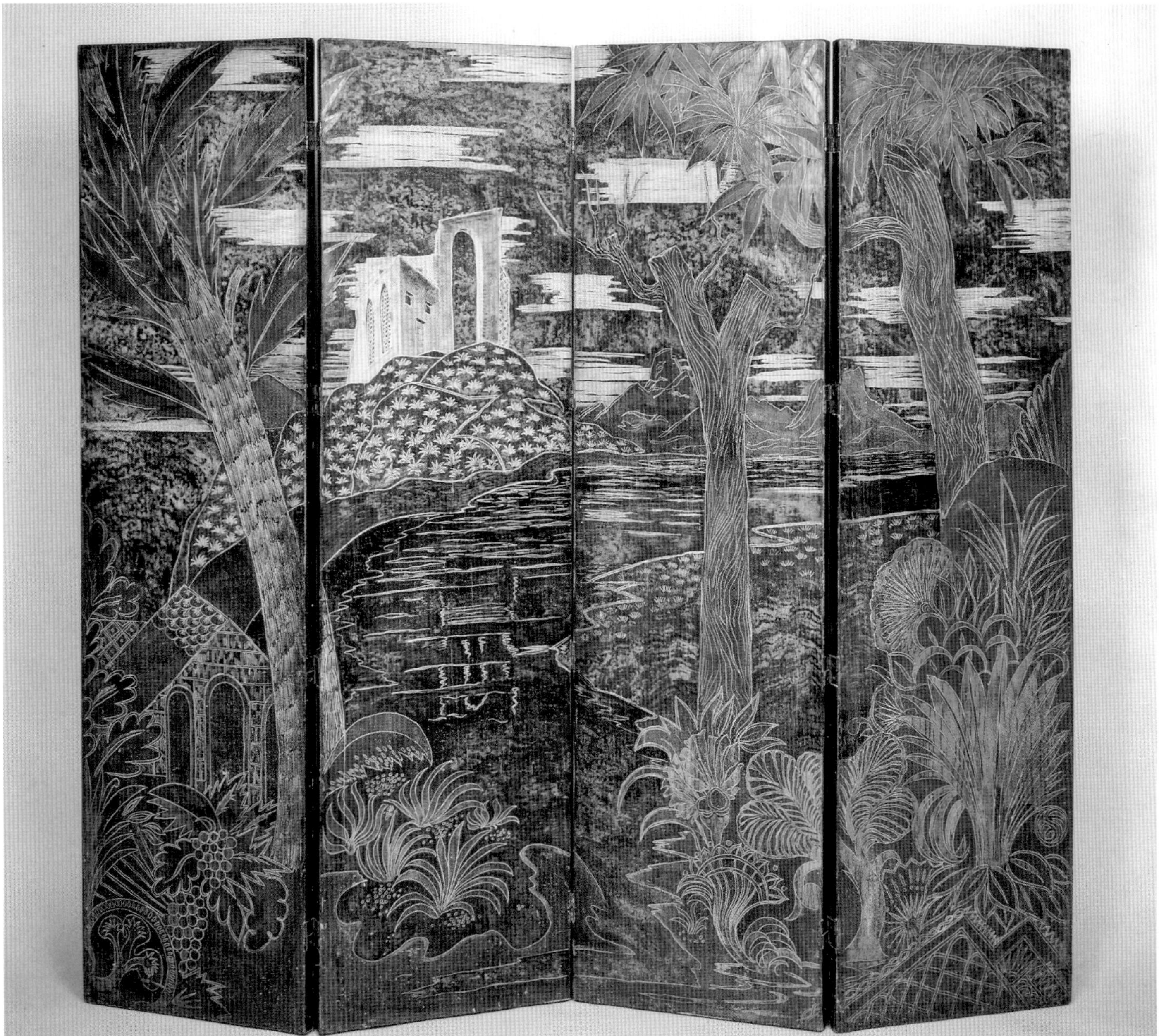

FIG 6 Max Kuehne, folding screen, 1924–28. Courtesy of Yale University Art Gallery, gift of Mr. and Mrs. Richard E. Kuehne

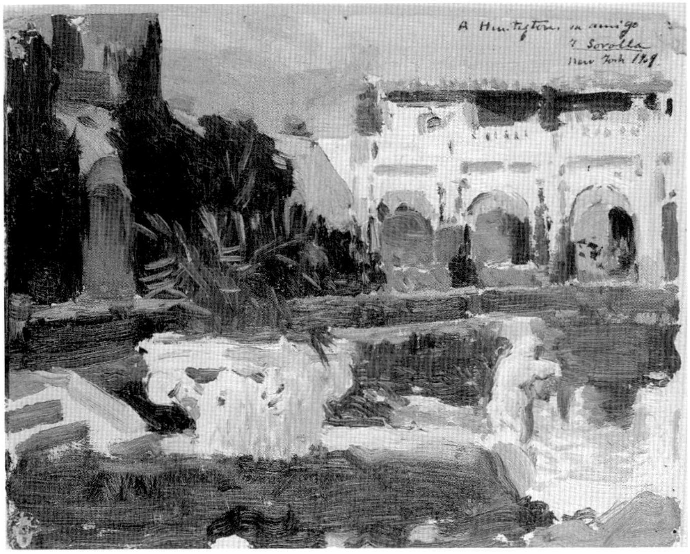

FIG 7 Joaquin Sorolla y Bastida, *A Sketch (Garden)*, 1909. Oil on canvas board, 7 × 9⅖ inches. Courtesy of the Hispanic Society of America

and Japanese design, and his furniture tended to be simplified Chinese Chippendale in style, particularly his tables. In his eclecticism, as in his admiration of things Spanish, Max Kuehne was very much a part of his time.

Americans continued to be interested in Spain through the late teens and 1920s. The Impressionist paintings of Joaquin Sorolla y Bastida (1863–1923) were much in vogue (fig. 7), and beginning in 1911, the artist painted a series of murals for the Hispanic Society. There were the books of Ernest Hemingway and others, particularly *The Sun Also Rises* (and later, in the 1930s, *For Whom the Bell Tolls*), and films starring Douglas Fairbanks, Jr., like *The Thief of Baghdad* and *The Mark of Zorro*. In architecture and interior design, the Spanish Colonial Revival style was almost as popular as American Colonial Revival (especially in movie theater architecture), with which it coexisted. One of the best-known and most discussed architects in the 1920s was Addison Mizner (1872–1933), who brought the Alhambra to Worth Avenue in Palm Beach, Florida, in 1924. Two years earlier, in Miami Beach, a "Spanish Village" had been re-created by the architect E. T. Roney.[16] The style was not limited to those areas of Spanish settlement in Florida, or California or the Southwest, however; clusters of Spanish Colonial-style houses appeared in various cities in the Northeast as well. The decorative forms of the style—metalwork, ceramic tile, and pottery, as well as furniture—were all part of a general trend in the 1920s for both residential and office space. (Charles and Maurice Prendergast, who sometimes collaborated on frame making with each other, also studied Spanish frames, beginning about 1907.) *The House Beautiful Furnishings Annual* for 1926 featured several sections devoted to Spanish furniture and reproductions of Spanish furniture, among other historicist styles.[17]

Although Max Kuehne's work in this medium was part of a general decorative movement at the time (as were the murals of painters Gardner Hale, Eugene Savage, William Palmer, and even the photographer Edward Steichen), the artist infused that work with an individual intensity, as well as a lyricism of color and line. Like his friend and colleague Charles Prendergast, Kuehne transcended the purely craft aspects of the medium to create works of art, according to critic Horace Wesley Ott, "on a par with his art as a landscape painter." In fact, works such as the framed three-paneled folding screen (*Floral Arrangement in Pink and Silver*, pl. 10) and the secretary he made for his personal use (pl. 17); or the carved and gilded horse (pl. 19) and the round coffee table (*Peacock and Foliage*, pl. 18), were not so much the products of a "second career" as an extension of a way of working in which all the parts fit together in the same way that one of his tables fit together. In 1921, one of Kuehne's armoires was included in an exhibition organized by the Architectural League of New York and held at The Metropolitan Museum of Art; and a number of the art dealers who carried his paintings sometimes showed his decorative work as well. The Montross Gallery, for example, included a chest in an exhibition in 1923; the Rehn Gallery exhibited an incised panel in 1927; and there was enough interest in this aspect of the artist's work to warrant an article in *International Studio* in 1926.[18]

Kuehne created the frames for most of his own paintings, and in his belief that the frame was an extension of the painting, he belongs to the tradition of artist-frame designers, a tradition that includes James McNeill Whistler, the architect Stanford White, and the painters Hermann Dudley Murphy in Boston, Arthur and Lucia Mathews in San Francisco, and Frederick Harer in Bucks County, Pennsylvania, with whom Kuehne became friendly in the late 1920s. The list also includes artists like John Marin, Walt Kuhn, and Louis Comfort Tiffany, but perhaps one of the most famous (and the most relevant to Kuehne) was Charles Prendergast (1863–1948; see William Adair's essay in this publication).[19]

Charles Prendergast, with the encouragement of his brother Maurice, began making frames around 1897, and by 1910 had achieved great success. He made frames for a number of works in the famous Armory Show in 1913, and a year later the Prendergast brothers moved to New York. Charles Prendergast, however, was interested in more

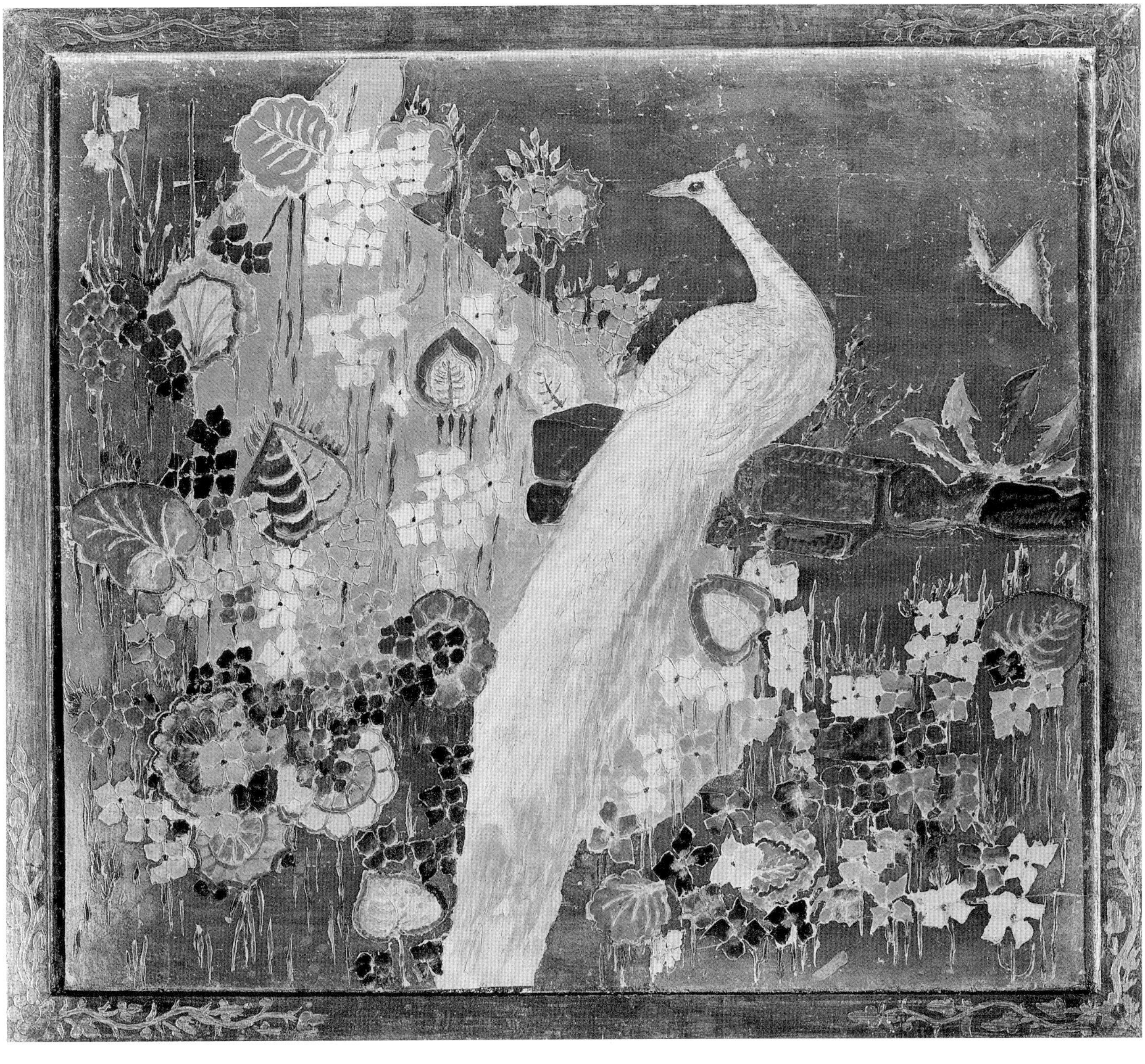

FIG 8 Max Kuehne, decorative incised panel *(Peacock and Flowers)*, n.d. Gessoed wood, watercolor, silver leaf, shellac, 28 × 31⅞ inches. Collection of Mrs. Theodore Lerner, Maryland

than frame making. In 1909 he wrote an article entitled "The Revival of Wood Carving," published in *House Beautiful*. He also made carved and painted gesso panels, the earliest of which was completed around 1912; chests and boxes as early as 1915; and sculptures beginning around 1912–14, one of which was included in an exhibition in New York in 1918.[20] Prendergast did not make as much furniture as Max Kuehne, and when he did, unlike Kuehne, he used ready-made pieces and then applied his designs. The gessoed and incised panels were another matter. These seemed to represent Prendergast's segue from making frames to making art. The form might have had some influence on Max Kuehne who adopted it himself later on, including Prendergast's use of an "engaged" frame—a raised edge of the same panel into which the image is carved or incised. Max Kuehne and Charles Prendergast probably met when the Kuehnes returned to New York from Spain in 1917. "Dick Kuehne does not remember Maurice, but knew 'Charlie' Prendergast, whom he described as gentle and easy-going."[21] Indeed, there is an air of gentleness and naive simplicity to the imagery in Prendergast's panels, imagery that is closer to his brother's work than to Kuehne's. Although Max Kuehne and Charles Prendergast both used the incised panel form and although many of their sources of inspiration, such as Persian miniatures and early Christian motifs, were similar, a comparison of their panels—for example, *Tree of Life* (pl. 4) and *Edge of the Cove* (pl. 12), by Kuehne, and *Figures (II)* by Prendergast (fig. 9)—reveals their differences. Naiveté and simplicity, a folk-art quality evident in Prendergast's work, is entirely absent from Kuehne's more sophisticated and stylish approach. What the two artists' panels do share, however, is a similarity in technique—in the use of incised or engraved, gilded, and painted gesso on a wood surface —"work," Prendergast once wrote, "done in gesso, the old Italian method."[22]

In Spain, according to Richard Kuehne, his father learned "the old Italian method" of frame making by buying old frames and examining their methods of construction and the carving and gilding. Unlike Charles Prendergast, who consulted the celebrated Renaissance manual *Il Libro Dell'Arte (The Craftsman's Handbook)* by Cennino D'Andrea Cennini, Max Kuehne was primarily self-taught (as his son says, "No one could teach my father anything!"). Richard Kuehne, who also works in the "old Italian method," owns two versions of the Cennini book, but he essentially learned the technique from his father.[23]

Richard describes the procedure Max Kuehne used in making his panels, furniture, and carvings—including the cocktail table *Primroses* (pl. 21) and the (now framed) three-paneled folding screen *White Flowers and Foliage* (pl. 3)—as follows. First, he would select a piece of wood such as redwood, a fine-grain dry wood that takes glue and gesso perfectly. He would then be ready to apply the gesso and proceed with his design. Gesso, a mixture of binder and filler, is used in gilding, a process in which a contiguous layer of gold leaf is applied to a wood surface (the term is also used here to include the use of silver and platinum leaf as well.) As discussed earlier, gesso has been used by artists for centuries as a ground, usually on wood panels, sometimes on canvas, because of the quality of the luminous pure white surface it produces. Gesso in this context, then, can be seen as a kind of metaphor for the "artist and craftsman."

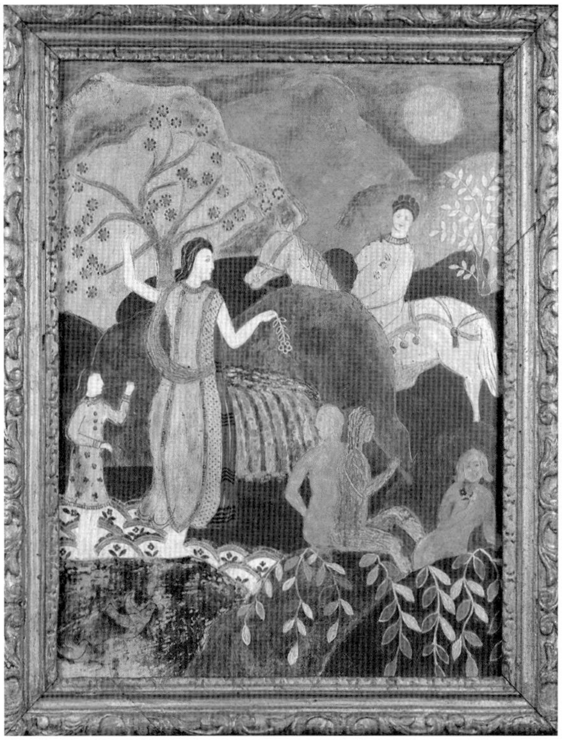

FIG 9
Charles Prendergast, *Figures (II)*, c. 1916–17. Oil and gold leaf on gessoed panel, 19½ × 16 inches. Baker/Pisano Collection

Kuehne used rabbit-skin glue as a binder, one of the strongest adhesives known, and the binder of choice for use in water-gilding frames since the beginnings of frame making. Kuehne also used this glue for his furniture. In preparation, the sheet (or sheets) of glue is soaked in water for four or five hours until it becomes a gelatin, then heated to between 60 and 90 degrees Fahrenheit. The filler is added to the glue while the glue is still warm. Later in his career Kuehne switched to a generic animal-hide glue, which was in granule form, easier to use, had a shorter soaking time, and could be stored for years. The filler used, called Gilder's Whiting, is composed of calcium carbonate the consistency of flour; when it sets it provides a brilliant white surface. In the process of applying the gesso, Kuehne would use five coats on the wood surface, smoothing it in between coats with a pumice stone. He later substituted open-mesh sandpaper, the kind used to smooth plaster walls. In the case of *Primroses*, it is likely that five coats of gesso were applied to the top, three coats to the stretchers, and two to the legs.

When the gesso was ready, Kuehne added on his designs with pencil— generally without preliminary drawings—sketching in a freehand manner similar to the way he worked on his paintings, in order to convey a sense of ease and spontaneity. Once he was satisfied with his design, it was incised or engraved into the gessoed surface, and a layer of bole (clay and binder) was spread on to receive the application of silver leaf (according to Richard Kuehne, his father did not use gold leaf in his furniture, but applied silver leaf covered by an orange shellac for a gold effect, a technique he learned by studying Spanish frames). Areas to be painted were generally left ungilded, although Kuehne often gilded everything and painted over the gilding in the manner of a Renaissance craftsman. His account books, owned by Mr. and Mrs. Richard Kuehne, indicate that he bought gold leaf in 1917, but presumably it was used only in his frames. He preferred silver leaf on his furniture because it allowed him more flexibility. He painted the areas containing color with ordinary watercolors, not tempera, contrary to what is indicated by Horace Wesley Ott and others. Neither Kuehne nor Prendergast used tempera of any kind; the watercolor pigment would mix with the binder and "strike" or soak into the gesso, bonding with it—much like the fresco technique—creating an insoluble surface.[24] In the course of finishing the piece, Kuehne shellacked the surface, sealing the color. Depending on the effect he wanted, he used either white or orange shellac. For the table he used orange shellac to make the silver leaf look gold; for the screen he used a white shellac in order to retain the silver effect. When the shellac had dried, a white "brush-flow" lacquer was applied and for the final finish coat, a mixture of turpentine, Japan Driers, and whiting was brushed on and wiped off, leaving the white to pick out and emphasize the incised outline (this part of the technique is more obvious in the screen *White Flowers and Foliage* than in the table *Primroses* (pls. 3, 21).[25]

The furniture styles Kuehne chose to use were almost as eclectic and historically oriented as the design motifs he adapted, although neither was chosen for historical accuracy or antiquarian interest, but to evoke a personal sense of the decorative. His first criterion was that, in the words of Horace Ott in 1926, "the piece offer adequate opportunity for decoration . . . requiring only that his model be excellent in line and that it possess large flat surfaces. And so, we find that one of his beds recalls Venice . . . another obviously owes its inspiration to that of Marie Antoinette . . . while perhaps his loveliest table is the Colonial tilt top variety."[26] Juliana Force's extensive furniture collection included a Colonial Revival-style table by Kuehne.[27] The artist's adaptation of chests also encompassed Spanish and Renaissance models and, along with the Chinese Chippendale style, which probably came later, he made and decorated simple round tables, such as *Peacock and Foliage* (pl. 18). A few of these tables were based on preparatory drawings.

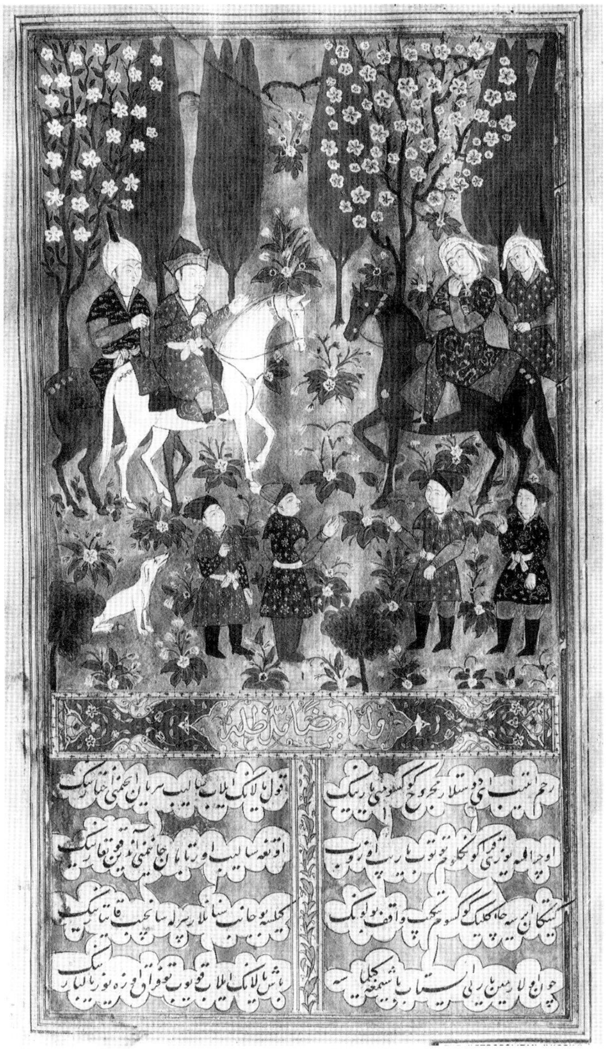

FIG 10 Persian painting on paper, from the manuscript of Diwan by Mir'Ali Shir Nawa'i. Fifteenth century, 9½ × 6 inches. Courtesy of The Metropolitan Museum of Art, gift of Alexander Smith Cochran, 1913

Although Kuehne created his designs in a spontaneous and free manner, he sometimes made delicate and elegant architectural drawings to show to architects or interior decorators. He also may have made these for Charles Gracie and Company, an interior design firm that specialized in special wallpapers and fabrics, some of which Kuehne used to line the drawers of chests. Like Charles Prendergast, Kuehne's motifs were drawn largely from Persian miniatures (fig. 10), but also Coptic designs, especially early on. Later, in the 1930s, in addition to the Coptic motifs, Far Eastern designs also became important. His favorite elements appear to be animals—dogs, leopards, deer, and birds, especially—along with flowers and foliage, the idea, perhaps being to represent Paradise (which is the word for garden in Persian). The delightful fire screen *Deer and Leopard in Landscape* (pl. 8), originally made as part of a bedroom set for members of the Whitney family, reflects a Persian interest through its depiction of animals in a tropical setting (and, because of its size, also evokes the flavor of a medieval French tapestry). The framed three-paneled screen *Floral Arrangement in Pink and Silver* (pl. 10) and the panel *Tree of Life* (pl. 4) show Kuehne's interest in the art of the Far East, and books on the subject were an important part of the artist's library. He owned, among other works, a much used book on Coptic textile designs, published by the Louvre; René Grousset's *Art of the Far East: Landscapes, Flowers, Animals*, published by Oxford University Press in 1936; and a series of exhibition catalogues on Japanese screen painting published by the Museum of Fine Arts Boston in the 1930s. The panel *Tree of Life*, with its dominant foreground tree and grasses, is reminiscent of the early-seventeenth-century Japanese artists Sotatsu and Korin. *Magnolia Screen*, a six-paneled screen in the collection of The Metropolitan Museum of Art attributed to the Sotatsu-Korin school, is strikingly similar to the design in Kuehne's panel (fig. 11). In his use of empty space and in the disposition of the forms of both *Floral*

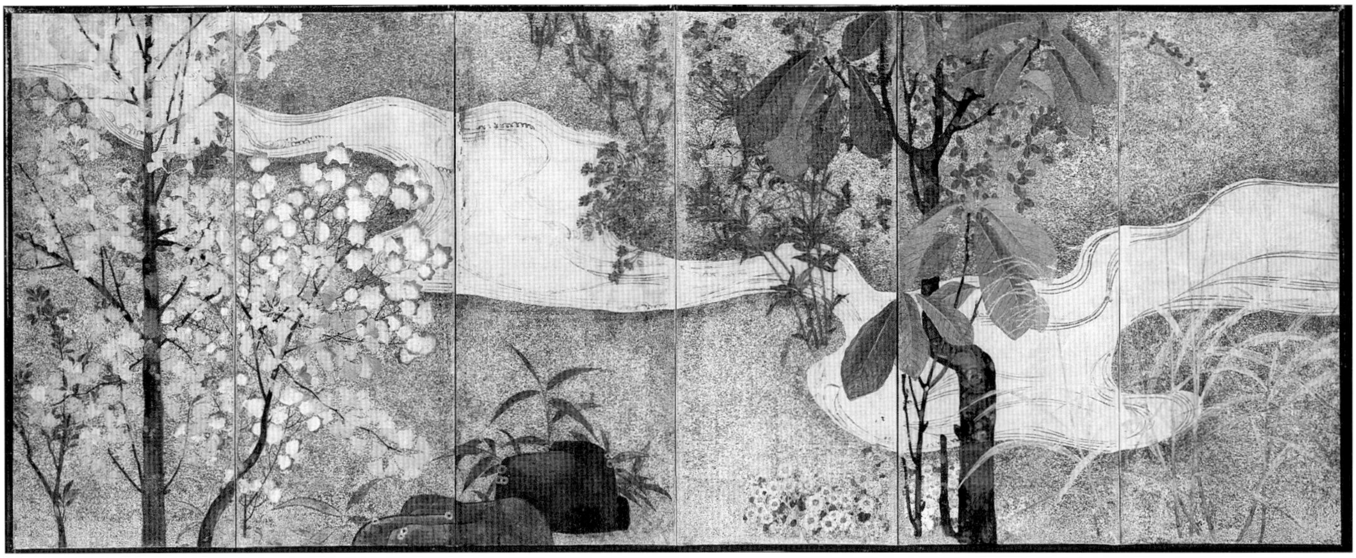

Arrangement in Pink and Silver and the double-sided three-paneled folding screen *Leaves and Grasses* (pl. 6), Kuehne conveys a very Japanese feeling similar to that of a pair of six-fold screens, *Autumn Grasses,* by an unknown mid-seventeenth-century Japanese painter, also in The Metropolitan Museum of Art (fig. 12).

FIG 11 Unidentified artist of the Sotatsu-Korin school, *Magnolia Screen,* Tokugawa Period (17–18th century). Six-paneled screen, colors on paper, 48 × 123 inches. Courtesy of The Metropolitan Museum of Art, Rogers Fund, 1915

In 1932, Kuehne presented a solo show of his furniture and eight of his screens at the Arden Gallery in New York, taking into account how his screens would look when folded (as can be seen in the two screens discussed above). It is clear that he had mastered the art of screen design, and in so doing he became part of a Far Eastern-inspired tradition that took hold in eighteenth-century France, became popular in the late nineteenth and the beginning of the twentieth century in the hands of Pierre Bonnard, among others, and became very fashionable in the 1920s and 1930s in both Europe and America, when even Thomas Hart Benton attempted it.[28]

During the 1930s, especially as the Depression deepened, Kuehne turned increasingly to his woodcarving and decorative work as a way to support his family. "My father survived this period," wrote Richard Kuehne, "by creating decorative screens, panels, sculpture, and furniture in gesso and silver leaf."[29] Although much of his furniture and carving was done in the 1930s and early 1940s, including the whimsical sculptures of a horse (reminiscent of carousel horse or children's rocking horses) and a pair of giraffes (pls. 16, 19), it is not always easy to date Max Kuehne's work, as the artist generally did not do so himself. Richard Kuehne has provided information and the account books provide some clues.

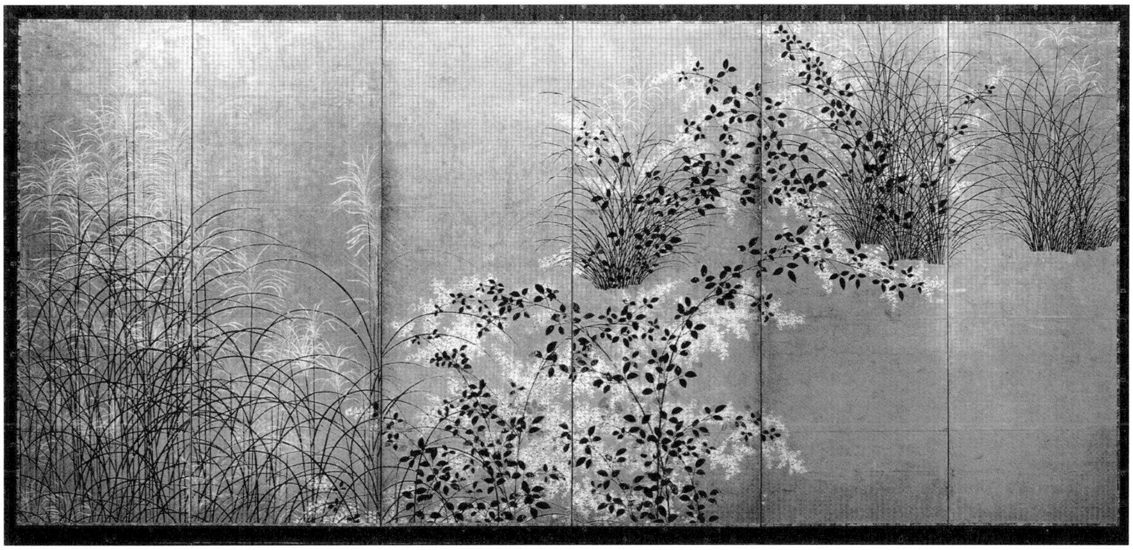

FIG 12 Unknown artist, *Autumn Grasses*, Early Edo Period (mid-17th century). Six-fold screen, colors on gold ground, 66½ × 144 inches. Courtesy of The Metropolitan Museum of Art, Purchase, Arthur Wiesenberger Foundation Gift, Louis V. Bell Fund, Dorothy Graham Bennett Fund, Pfeiffer and Seymour Funds, 1972

The account books also indicate the artist's sources of patronage. From Archer M. Huntington, through A. E. Gallatin and Dr. Albert C. Barnes, to Gertrude Vanderbilt Whitney and, especially, Juliana Force, Max Kuehne was fortunate in having sympathetic and consistent patronage. The earliest mention of his furniture is in 1917 when his account books show that he had made a cabinet, credenza, and a "modern commode." In 1918 he built two bookcases for Juliana Force. That same year he was included in a group exhibition at the Whitney Studio Club, together with John Sloan, Reynolds Beal, William Glackens, Stuart Davis, and Paul Manship. Gertrude Vanderbilt Whitney had become a major patron of American artists, both on her own and through Juliana Force, who would become the first director of the Whitney Museum. Mrs. Whitney provided support, not only to Max Kuehne but also to artists like John Sloan, Edward Hopper, Stuart Davis, and Rockwell Kent at a crucial time in their careers.[30] Richard Kuehne asserts, "Among those . . . who gave him encouragement was Juliana Force . . . whose support of artists and the cause of American art in the Depression years cannot be overestimated."[31] Mrs. Force had been an active patron before the Depression as well. In 1924, according to the account books, she commissioned a table, a book stand, and a serving tray; also in that year Kuehne made a panel, two trays, and three cigarette boxes for Mrs. Whitney. In 1927 he constructed a bed and table for Mrs. Whitney Miller (undoubtedly through Gertrude Whitney). From 1917 through the 1930s, Gertrude Whitney and Juliana Force were Kuehne's most important patrons; he even applied palladium leaf to Mrs. Whitney's sculpture

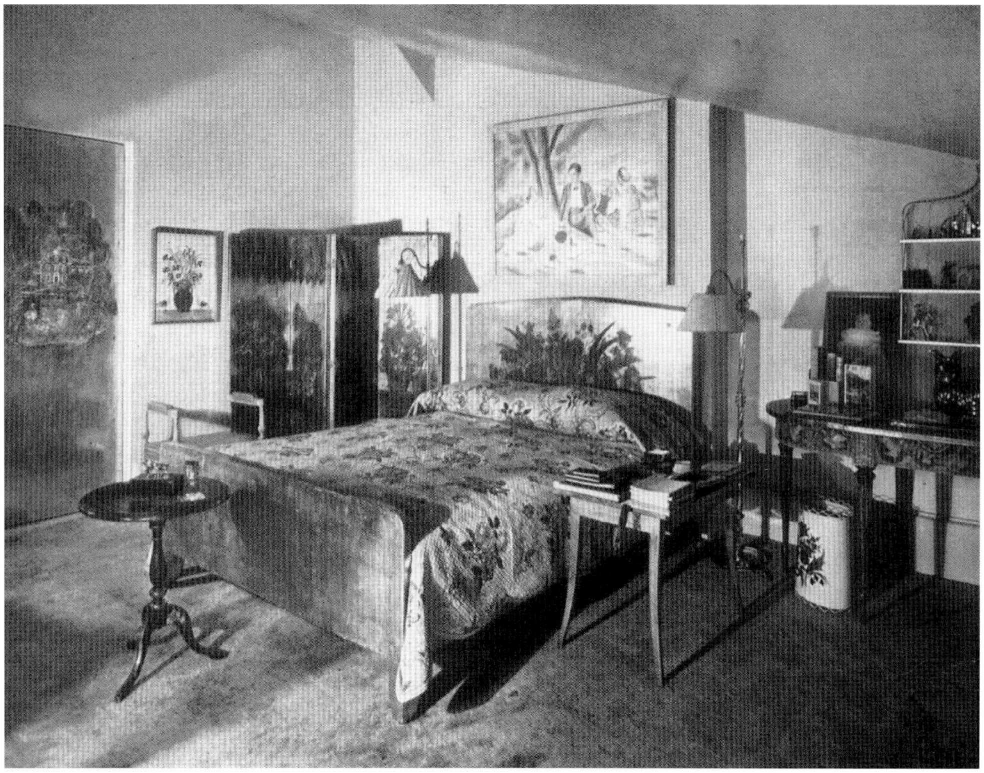

FIG 13 Juliana Force's bedroom, decorated with Max Kuehne furniture, 1937. The door, bed frame and headboard, and folding screen are all gessoed works in wood by Kuehne. Photograph from *Country Life*, April 1937, courtesy of Avis Berman

commissioned for the New York World's Fair of 1939, the base of which was designed by R. Buckminster Fuller. Between 1929 and 1931, Juliana Force commissioned 163 frames from Kuehne. Her collection during the 1930s also included Kuehne's serving tray *Yellow Poenies* (pl. 13). An article in *Country Life* for April 1937 described the decoration of her apartment, which contained a Kuehne painting, a bed, two tables, a folding screen, and a door: "The bedroom contains many examples of gesso work by Mr. Max Kuehne, one of the few experts in this art"[32] (figs. 13–15).

Another interesting early patron was Albert Eugene Gallatin (1881–1952). A collector, critic, and late in life, a painter, A. E. Gallatin was heir to a banking family. His great-grandfather was Secretary of the Treasury under Presidents Jefferson and Madison and also Minister to France and England. Gallatin began collecting books and posters at an early age. He gradually began to assemble a more modern collection; after 1927 his taste shifted toward European Modernism, 160 works of which he bequeathed to the Philadelphia Museum of Art in 1952.[33] At one time his collection

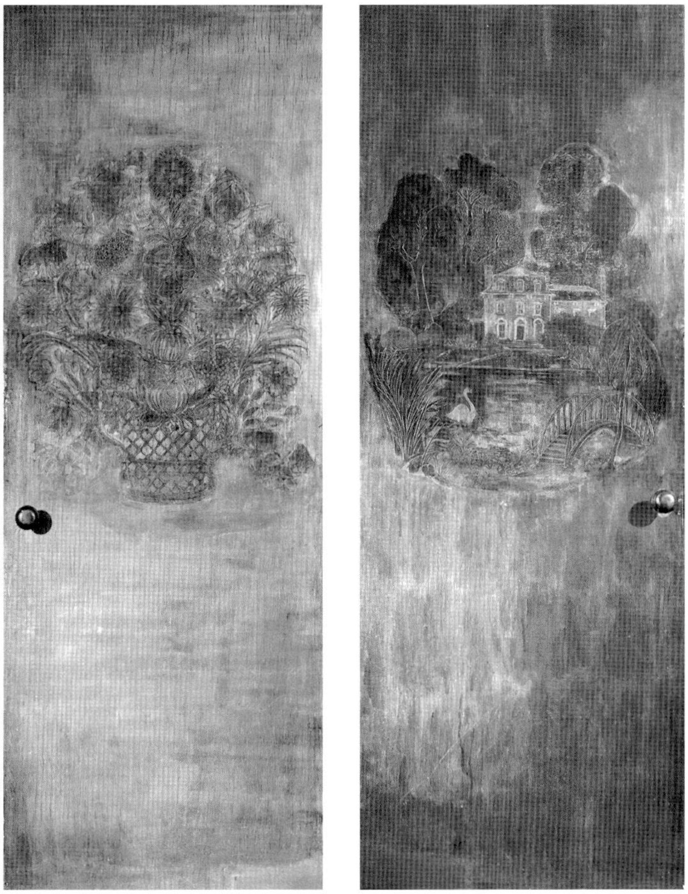

FIG 14 (left) Door with double-sided incised painting (*Bouquet of Flowers* and *Barley Sheaf Farm*), mid 1930s. Gessoed wood, watercolor, silver leaf, lacquer, 78 × 30 1/2 inches. Private collection

FIG 15 (right) Preparatory studies for *Bouquet of Flowers* and *Barley Sheaf Farm*

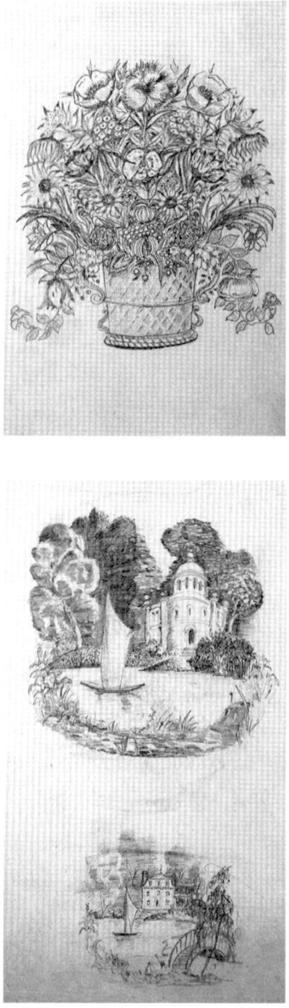

included at least ten paintings and four or five frames by Kuehne; he also supported the artist by writing about him, and in an article of 1919 for *International Studio* called him "one of the half a dozen or so most important landscape men in America."[34]

The year that Gallatin published the article, Kuehne's account books listed a chest made for "Barnes." Of all Max Kuehne's patrons, Dr. Albert C. Barnes (1872–1951), was the most eccentric and perhaps the most egotistical. His collection, however, was astonishing, especially the holdings in classic modern French painting, from Renoir to Cézanne to Matisse.[35] Barnes liked Kuehne and he liked his work; in a series of letters to the artist between 1921 and 1923, during the period when his celebrated Barnes Foundation was being built in Merion, Pennsylvania, Barnes offered Kuehne support, both financial and moral. He even gave the artist some sharp advice on how to auction his paintings ("If you only had a friend or two to push up the prices at the start & get from under when the price gets near market, it would be a good thing."),[36] and subjected Kuehne to his own brand of "pop" psychology, offering corrections to what he saw as the artist's faulty work habits (in a letter of May 4, 1921). But he also ordered "a couple of chests" to "keep you in the running until things turn your way."[37] In that same letter, of February 2, 1923, he wrote," It ought to interest your painter friends who look down on you, to know that your 20 x 24 Spanish landscape & two small ones, will hang in the gallery of the Foundation holding its own with some good paintings by men internationally famous."

The letters Barnes sent to Max Kuehne were written to the artist in New York, a New York that was changing rapidly; it was fast becoming the city of skyscrapers that so fascinated later European artist-émigrés. It was the New York of the Art Deco architecture of the Chrysler Building (1926–30), the McGraw-Hill Building (1929–30), the Empire State Building (1929–31), and finally, Rockefeller Center, built between 1927 and 1935. Although the Kuehnes lived at 104 East 57th Street from 1932 to 1944, and from 1944 to 1968 at 25½ East 61st Street, much of Max Kuehne's carving and furniture was executed on Cape Ann, in the fishing village of Rockport, Massachusetts to which Kuehne had been going every summer since 1925.

As he grew older, Kuehne stayed in Rockport longer and longer before returning to the city. After Spain, Cape Ann became the geographical location most important to his work. Cape Ann had been attracting artists ever since FitzHugh Lane established a studio in Gloucester in 1847. "Nearly all the leading names in American art," wrote Max Kuehne's friend, the illustrator and cartoonist Harrison Cady, "have at some time or other . . . been temporary or permanent residents of either Gloucester, Annisquam . . . or Rockport."[38] Rockport itself was the most often painted subject in the United States. The New England topography of Cape Ann featured ocean vistas and white church spires, fishing shanties as well as distinctive architecture, all of which were unified by not only the presence of the sea but, as in Spain, the pervasive clarity of the light; "a brilliance of light," wrote Kuehne's acquaintance, Stuart Davis, "greater than I have ever seen."[39] Max Kuehne first rented a summer residence on Bearskin Neck, a mini-peninsula located at the harbor on Sandy Bay and once the site of fishermen's shacks that had been the commercial center of Rockport for over 150 years. In 1937, Kuehne was able to buy a summer residence at 29 Marmion Way, a hilltop area overlooking the harbor, and in 1953 the Kuehnes moved closer to the center of town, to 14 Gott Street, a converted barn and former studio of the artists Jonas Lie and Stanley Woodward, which Kuehne owned until his death in 1968.

Although Kuehne devoted much of his time to his furniture making and carving in the 1930s, he did take up etching and he kept painting. "Father continued to paint," wrote his son in "A Reminiscence," "but only during those intervals that he could spare from his work in gesso." Kuehne learned etching, the medium of Rembrandt, Whistler, and Mary Cassatt, from one of the best printmakers of his day, John Taylor Arms (1887–1953), whose *Handbook of Print Making and Print Makers* (1934) was influential. One of Kuehne's early etchings, of the famous First Universalist Church in Gloucester, built in 1804, was used as an illustration in James B. Connelly's book *The Port of Gloucester* (1940), along with four other etchings of Gloucester by Kuehne (fig. 15). Like his etchings and like the work of most of his fellow painters in the Rockport Art Association, Kuehne's painting remained grounded in Realism during this period, despite (or maybe because of) the radical changes in the art world of New York. From the late 1940s onward, however, his style changed completely. He adopted a pointillist method and after 1948 fell under the spell of the great French painter Pierre Bonnard (1867–1947), whom, Richard Kuehne said, "he greatly admired for his color." Max Kuehne came to appreciate the French artist late in his career and "a retrospective [memorial] exhibition of Bonnard's painting held at the Museum of Modern Art [in 1948] did provide the stimulus for a complete departure from the concept and style of his early painting."[40] The painting *Flowers in White Pitcher*, of circa 1960 (pl. 35), with its glowing and resonant color, reflects that departure. In addition, the gilded and polychromed frame, an extension of the painting itself, mirrors the artist's lifelong ability to combine power of expression with an equally strong, yet elegant decorative sensibility. The frames supplied a link to the sculptures and panels. In his furniture and folding screens Kuehne found a way to achieve a balance that transcends both medium and category, in the words of the contemporary ceramist Wayne Higby (b. 1943), to "locate an additional area of expression."[41] That additional area is arrived at not only through extraordinary skill and consummate technique but also through "a dignity and sincerity of expression which is characteristic of the honest craftsman and artist.[42]

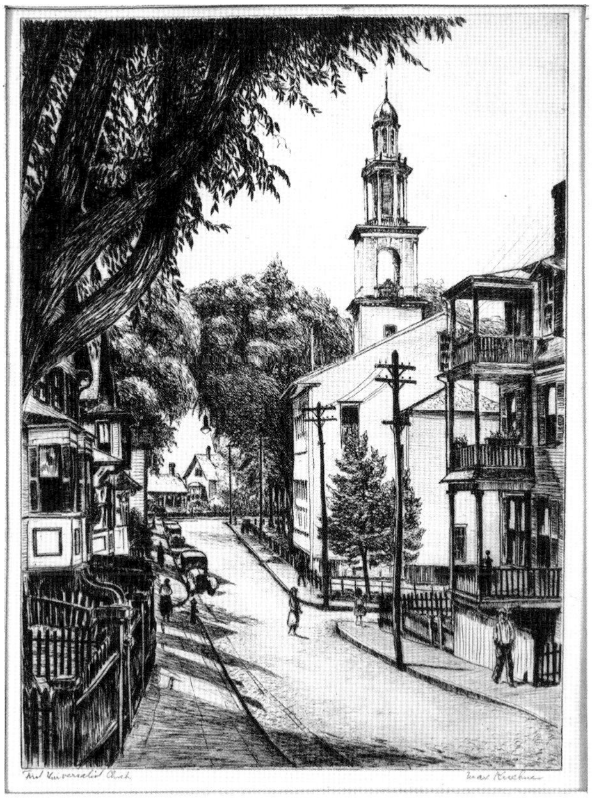

FIG 15 Max Kuehne, *First Universalist Church*, Gloucester, c. 1930s. Etching. Collection of the Cape Ann Historical Association. Photograph courtesy of Mr. and Mrs. Richard Kuehne

NOTES AND BIBLIOGRAPHY

The citations in these notes also serve as a bibliography. I have drawn heavily on two sources: Sharon Ann Worley, *Max Kuehne: Paintings, Furniture, Sculpture* (Gloucester, Mass.: Cape Ann Historical Museum, 1997), and Richard Kuehne, "A Reminiscence," in *The Early Paintings of Max Kuehne* (New York: Hirschl & Adler Galleries, Inc., 1972). I have also relied on the other writings of Richard Kuehne, the artist's son, and a very pleasant and stimulating interview I conducted with him on January 3 and 4, 2001, in Rockport, Massachusetts, as well as many telephone conversations since.

1 From an interview with Max Kuehne by Ann Beal, late 1950s, as related to the author, January 10, 2001, Philadelphia; Horace Wesley Ott, "Max Kuehne's Furniture in Gesso," *International Studio* 84 (July 1926), p. 71.

2 Max Kuehne also taught his son and grandson the technique of wood carving and of creating incised and gilded furniture in gesso.

3 Interview with Richard Kuehne by the author. See also Worley, *Max Kuehne*, pp. 6–7.

4 *Baedeker's United States, Handbook for Travellers* (Leipzig, Germany: Karl Baedeker, 1899).

5 Richard Kuehne, "A Reminiscence."

6 Worley, *Max Kuehne*, p. 9.

7 Interview with Richard Kuehne by the author.

8 Richard Kuehne, "A Reminiscence."

9 M. Elizabeth Boone, "Sol y Sombra: American Artists Explore the Sunlight and Shadows of Spain," in *España: American Artists and the Spanish Experience* (New York: Hollis Taggart Galleries, 1999), p. 15; for a discussion of Max Kuehne, see pp. 80–81.

10 Richard Kuehne, "A Reminiscence."

11 See Denys Sutton, "A Munificent Hispanophile," *Apollo*, April 1972, pp. 2–5.

12 A. E. Gallatin, *Max Kuehne: Sixteen Reproductions of the Artist's Work* (New York: E. P. Dutton & Co., 1924), p. 7.

13 Richard Kuehne, "A Reminiscence;" Frickenhausen-am-Main was Margaret [Gresser] Kuehne's hometown in Germany from which she eloped with Max Kuehne in 1913.

14 For a discussion of the Kuehne family's New York residences, see Worley, *Max Kuehne*, note 21, p. 33.

15 Richard Kuehne, "A Reminiscence."

16 See Christina Orr, *Addison Mizner: Architect of Dreams and Realities* (Palm Beach, Fla.: Norton Gallery of Art, 1977). See also Barbara Baer Capitman, *Deco Delights: Preserving the Beauty and Joy of Miami Beach Architecture* (New York: E. P. Dutton, 1988), pp. 64–65.

17 Fiske Kimball, "Introduction,"*The House Beautiful Furnishings Annual 1926, A Comprehensive and Practical Manual for the Guidance of All Who Seek Comfortable and Attractive Homes* (Boston: The Atlantic Monthly Company, 1925), pp. 36, 63, 67, 77.

18 Worley, *Max Kuehne*, p. 22; see Ott, "Max Kuehne's Furniture in Gesso," pp. 71–75.

19 See Suzanne Smeaton, "American Picture Frames of the Arts and Crafts Period, 1870–1920," *Antiques* 136 (November 1989), pp. 1124–1937.

20 See catalogue section in Nancy Mowll Mathews, *The Art of Charles Prendergast: From the Collections of the Williams College Museum of Art & Mrs. Charles Prendergast*, with an essay by Marion Goethals (Williamstown, Mass.: Williams College Museum of Art, 1993), p. 62. See also Carol Derby, "Charles Prendergast's Frames: Reuniting Design & Craftsmanship," in Carol Derby et al, *The Prendergasts and the Arts and Crafts Movement: The Art of American Decoration and Design, 1890–1920* (Williamstown, Mass.: Williams College Museum of Art, 1989), pp. 29–43.

21 Interview with Richard Kuehne by Carol Clark, of Williams College Museum of Art, June 2, 1984; my thanks to Nancy Mowll Mathews for sending me a copy of the transcript.

22 Quoted in Marion M. Goethals, "My Work Is Done in Gesso, the Old Italian Method," in Mathews, *The Art of Charles Prendergast*, p. 39.

23 Written in the fourteenth century, *Il Libro Dell'Arte* has been translated into French and German as well as English. In English it can be found under the titles *The Book of the Art of Cennino Cennini: A Contemporary Practical Treatise on Quattrocento Painting, Translated from the Italian, with Notes on Mediaeval Art Methods*, by Lady

Christina J. Herringham (London, 1899); or *The Craftsman's Handbook*, by Daniel V. Thompson, Jr. (New Haven, Conn.: Yale University Press, 1933). It is probably one of the first "how-to" manuals in art history, written by an artist for artists.

24 Undated letter from Nancy Mowll Mathews to the author regarding Charles Prendergast and the use of tempera: "We feel now that he did not use a traditional technique [egg or casein tempera], but his 'tempera' is merely opaque watercolor."

25 Interview with Richard Kuehne, to whom my thanks goes for spending an infinite amount of time with me in his studio patiently explaining this process. See also Grace Baggot, "Understanding the Binder in Gesso," *Picture Frame Magazine*, September 2000, with thanks to Richard Kuehne for bringing this article to my attention.

26 Ott, "Max Kuehne's Furniture in Gesso," p. 72.

27 See Avis Berman, *Rebels on Eighth Street: Juliana Force and the Whitney Museum of American Art* (New York: Atheneum, MacMillan Publishing Co., 1990), p. 2.

28 See Michael Komenecky et al, *The Folding Image* (New Haven, Conn.: Yale University Art Gallery, 1984); see also Joan Stanley Baker, *Japanese Art, World of Art Series* (London and New York: Thames and Hudson, 1990).

29 Richard Kuehne, "A Reminiscence."

30 Worley, *Max Kuehne*, p. 10.

31 Richard Kuehne, "A Reminiscence."

32 "Modern Interpretation of Victorian,"*Country Life*, April 1937, p. 22, collection of Avis Berman; my thanks to Ms. Berman for bringing this to my attention.

33 See Gail Stavitsky, "The A. E. Gallatin Collection: an Early Adventure in Modern Art," *Philadelphia Museum of Art Bulletin*, winter/spring 1994, nos. 379–80, pp. 5–47.

34 Quoted in Worley, *Max Kuehne*, pp. 12–13; see also idem, note 32, p. 34, for a complete list of Gallatin's publications on Kuehne.

35 In addition to the French artists in his Foundation, Barnes also collected the work of a significant number of American artists, mostly watercolors by painters such as the Prendergasts, Charles Demuth, and John Marin, as well as Max Kuehne's paintings and furniture.

36 Letter, Albert C. Barnes to Max Kuehne, December 12, 1922. Eight letters from Barnes to Kuehne (there are no letters from Kuehne to Barnes) are preserved in the Kuehne Archives at Syracuse University, New York, along with newspaper clippings, articles, and photographs by Peter Juley.

37 Letter, Albert C. Barnes to Max Kuehne, February 2, 1923.

38 [Walter] Harrison Cady, "Art Comes to Cape Ann," in Kitty Parsons Recchia, *Artists of the Rockport Art Association* (Rockport, Mass.: Rockport Art Association, 1989), p. 9. First published in 1940. Max Kuehne listed p. 138, pictured with his sculpture *(Horse)*, p. 74.

39 Quoted in Richard J. Boyle, "Charles Saelis Kaelin and the Cape Ann Art Colony," in Carol Lowrey and Richard J. Boyle, *Dialogues with Nature: Works by Charles Saelis Kaelin (1858–1929)* (New York: Spanierman Gallery, 1990), p. 35; for an additional bibliography on Cape Ann artists, see notes, pp. 40–41.

40 Richard Kuehne, "A Reminiscence."

41 Quoted in Richard J. Boyle, "Landscapes of Meaning: Images of Landscape in the Art of Wayne Higby," in *Landscape and Memory: the Art of Wayne Higby* (Helsinki: Museum of Art and Design; and Philadelphia: Helen Drutt, 1999), p. 11.

42 Ott, "Max Kuehne's Furniture in Gesso," p. 75.

ACKNOWLEDGMENTS

The following people have been more than helpful and encouraging in the organization of this exhibition and its catalogue: Mr. and Mrs. Richard Kuehne; Ann Beal; Fred Baker; Avis Berman; Marion M. Goethals, Associate Director, and Nancy Mowll Mathews, Eugene Prendergast Curator, Williams College Museum of Art; M. P. Naud, Hirschl & Adler Galleries; and Kirsten Olds and Cynthia Seibels, Hollis Taggart Galleries.

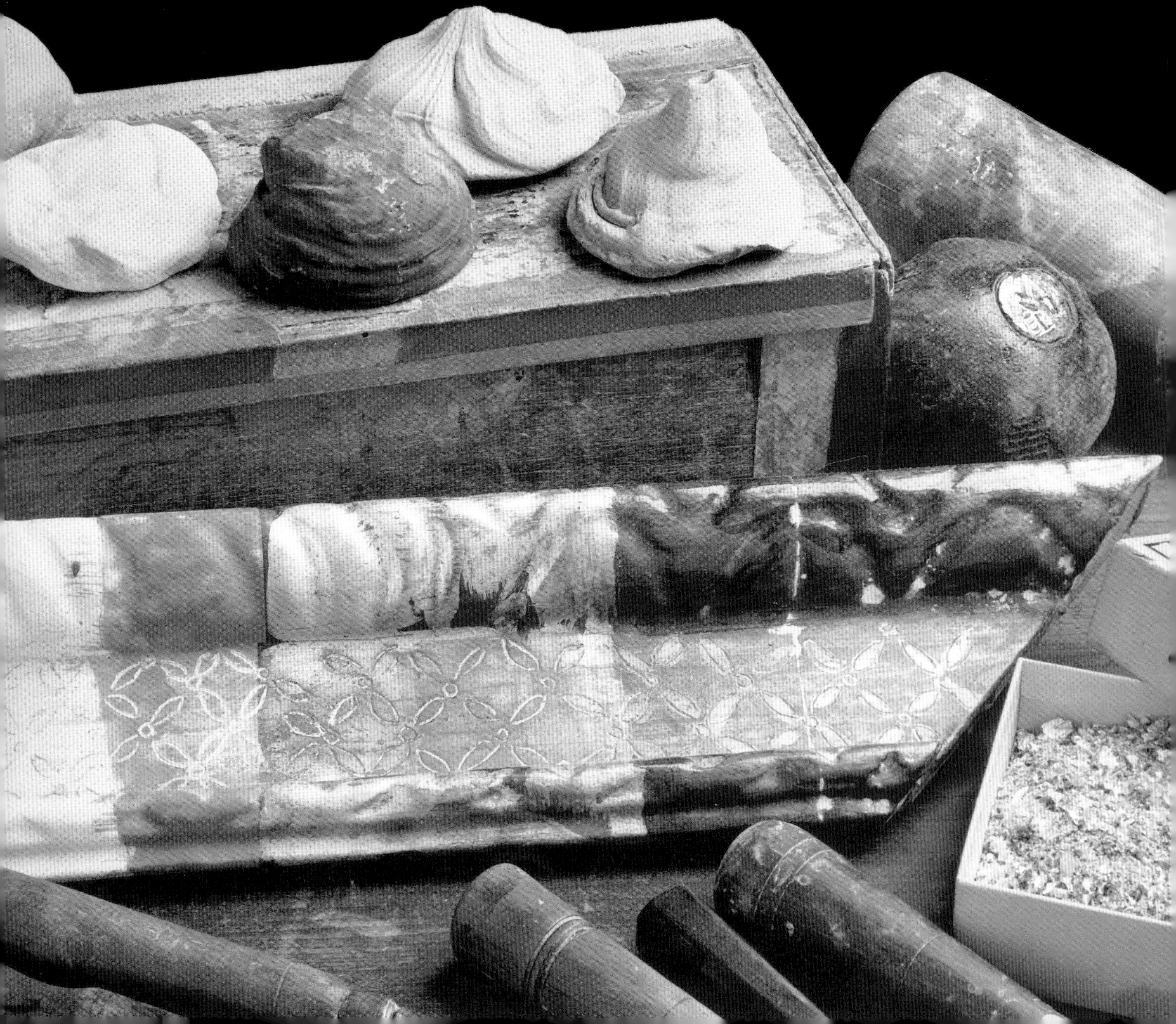

Sample of gilding materials
with cassetta molding.

Max Kuehne

FRAMES

WILLIAM B. ADAIR

For a more complete definition of framing terms and techniques, seen the Glossary on p. 81.

In the study of frames, comprehending what one sees is a difficult task, especially because the materials and techniques that are used in making them are often arcane. It is rare, even for experts, to contemplate a frame without some confusion. Understanding the basic processes and materials, such as the kinds of wood, methods of corner construction, composition, types of gesso and bole, and a variety of other gilding and toning techniques, can greatly enhance the appreciation of the collector and the historian.

Historically, most artists were interested in the frames surrounding their paintings.[1] The creation of a harmonious relationship between the frame and the painting was a means for an artist to set him- or herself apart, as well as controlling the presentation of the artwork to the public. James McNeill Whistler (1834–1903) was among the first American painters to move away from the Victorian penchant for superfluous design and ornamentation. His frames were simple by comparison and were often toned and painted to blend with the subtle tonalist color schemes used in his paintings.[2] Later in his career, Whistler further simplified his frames by omitting painted decoration, while emphasizing the molding in a dramatic series of three interlocking profiles of classical reeding, thereby setting the trend for the modernist aesthetic.

Like many American painters, Max Kuehne was influenced by Whistler. Kuehne, however, went one step further than Whistler, for he not only designed his own frames but carved and gilded them as well. Kuehne found inspiration in the study of antiques during his numerous trips to Europe, beginning in 1910. He purchased antique frames, rugs, and other furnishings, absorbing their finely ornamented patterns as inspiration for his frames and furniture designs (figs. 1, 2).

Kuehne developed a personal style that is clearly recognizable: a "cassetta" profile with an incised design created by using a special gesso-cutting technique.[3] The

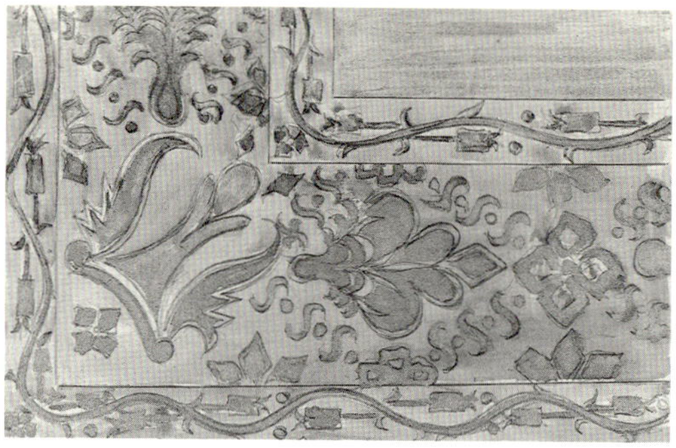

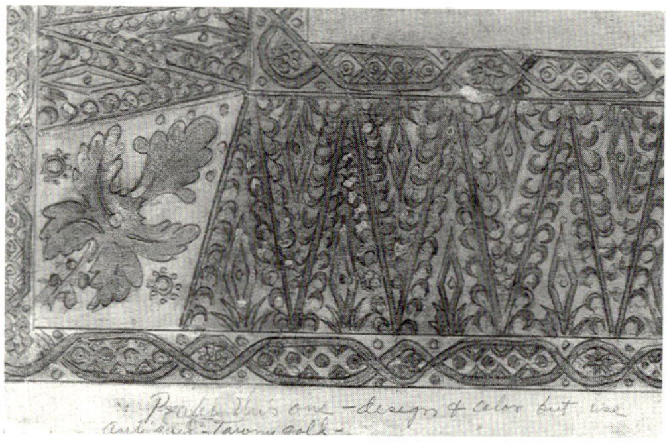

FIG 1 (far left) Circa seventeenth-century Spanish frame, purchased by Max Kuehne during one of his trips to Spain. Collection of Mr. and Mrs. Richard Kuehne

FIG 2 (left, top and bottom) Border designs for furniture made by Max Kuehne, c. 1920.

surface design was composed of an engraved flower and diamond shape, a lotus flower and circle, or sometimes just a plain flower. In other frames the artist would carve a "hazzle," or zigzag pattern, on the outer rim and a slightly irregular pattern on the inner edge. He usually used silver leaf, toned or oxidized with various colors, which resulted in a "tawny" gold effect with an exquisite antique patina.

Kuehne's frame work has often been confused with that of Charles Prendergast. Although their styles are similar, Kuehne's carving was precise and methodical, whereas Prendergast's was more loose and lyrical. Kuehne and Prendergast both survived the Depression working as artists, partly because of their skills in gilding and frame making. Having learned and mastered the craft of carving and water gilding, Kuehne and Prendergast created panels, screens, mirrors, furniture, and other decorative objects. All of these were made using traditional techniques and styles handed down from the Renaissance. Kuehne's designs may have been based on traditional motifs, but his inspiration came from a variety of sources, such as Persian miniatures or even embossed leather work, prevalent in the richly embellished interiors found in Spain where the artist lived for several years.[4] He possessed a highly refined aesthetic

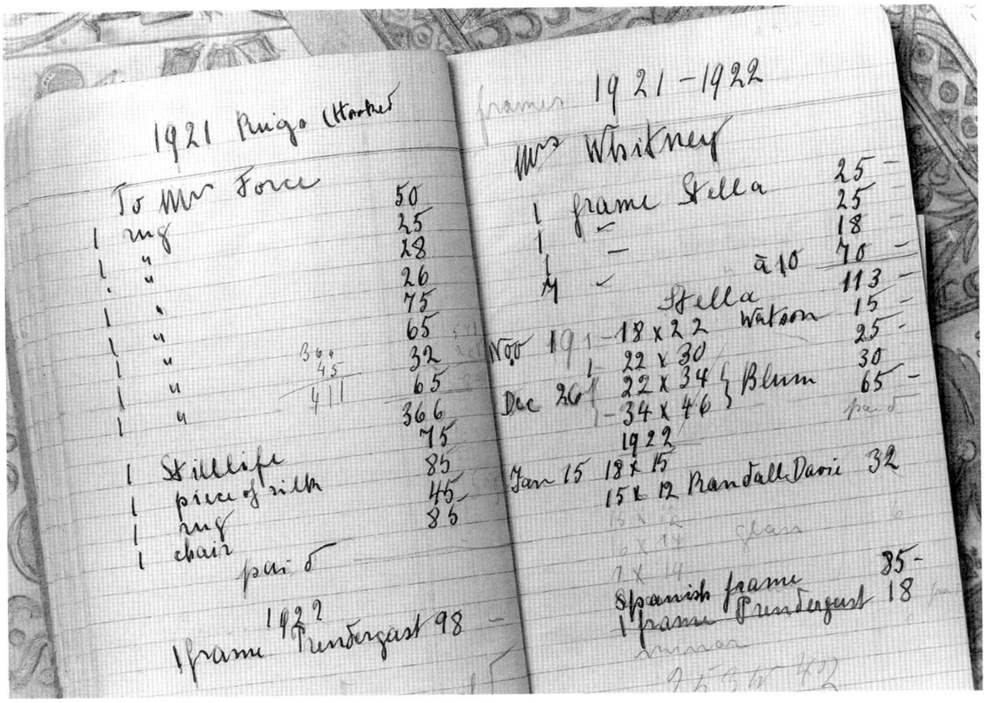

FIG 3 Max Kuehne, order book, 1921–22.

appreciation of subtle patinas and sophisticated design. His style, while distinctive, was still very much a part of the Arts and Crafts aesthetic.[5]

Kuehne made frames for institutions such as the precursor to the Whitney Museum of American Art, the Barnes Foundation, and the Hispanic Society, and artist friends like Rockwell Kent, Charles Prendergast, and William Glackens. Glackens once made the comment, "Every artist suffers from a chronic lack of suitable frames."[6] Charles Prendergast held Kuehne's work in such high esteem that when he received more commissions than he could handle, he would sub-contract the work to Kuehne (fig. 3).[7]

The most distinguishing characteristic of a Kuehne frame is the incised or sgraffito floral designs that are scratched through the leaf, exposing the white gesso underneath and creating a white border around the designs similar to the panel techniques used by Charles Prendergast. To produce this effect, the artist used a specially tooled and filed nail, mounted into a handle. It provided a contrast to the darkened and scumbled tones of the frame's surface, without overpowering the painting. Typically, Kuehne water-gilded with silver leaf, creating a burnished and matte surface. He would oxidize the silver leaf with a sulphur compound that instantly turned the metal into a subtle spectrum of iridescent pinks, greens, and blues on a gun-metal gray background, punctuated with an occasional flash of silver. The leaf would be selectively rubbed away to expose the color of the bole underneath, which was typically a brick shade. Kuehne also painted the sides of his frames with the same red bole instead of leafing them. The entire surface was then sealed with a lacquer, and a light stipple of white gesso was applied to selected areas of the "hazzle" carving along both the inner edge and outer rim. In some frames, Kuehne would paint selective areas with a gamboge and dragonsblood varnish to turn the silver visually into gold.[8] While most artisans signed the back of their frames at this time, it was not typical for Kuehne to do so, although there are some instances in which the initials "MK" appear on the back (such as *Still Life with Flowers,* pl. 34).

FIG 4 Max Kuehne. Cassetta frame. Hand-carved pine, gesso, red bole, incised and oxidized silver leaf with gamboge. Collection of Mr. and Mrs. Richard Kuehne.

This classic Italian cassetta frame is perhaps one of Kuehne's most successful frame designs. The sgraffito on the panel of the frame was drawn freehand on the surface. The silver is abraded to expose the bole, and a thin white glaze is scumbled into the crevices.

Kuhene was acutely aware of the fundamental concept that the proper frame can greatly enhance a painting.[9] The color, shape, texture, and luminosity of a frame, when carefully balanced with the artwork, can show the painting to its best advantage. He considered each frame he made integral to the painting. Today, Kuehne's frames are much sought after as works of art in their own right and can be found in museums, including the Art Institute of Chicago and the Memorial Art Gallery in Rochester, in addition to many other public and private collections (fig. 4).[10]

NOTES

1 Early in the nineteenth century, the artist Charles Willson Peale (1741–1827) stated, "I expect you will want a frame for it, as I suppose you cannot get them made in Kentucky in good workmanship. Prices of frames are various, in proportion to the quantity of gilding. . . . 10 dollars may be the price of a tolerable handsome frame—You can order one even cheaper, but a good picture deserves a good frame, and a bad picture may sometimes preserve its place longer by having a handsome frame. . . ." Charles Willson Peale to Alfred William Grayson, March 7, in Lillian B. Miller, ed., *The Collected Papers of Charles Willson Peale and His Family: A Microfiche Edition* (Millwood, N. Y., 1980). I am grateful to Lillian Miller, former editor of the Smithsonian's Peale Papers, for drawing my attention to this citation.

2 Whistler wrote to a collector on January 18, 1873, "I wish this to be clearly stated in Paris, that I am the inventor of all this kind of decoration in color in the frames, that I may not have a lot of clever little Frenchmen trespassing on my ground . . . many have painted on their frames, but never with real purpose or knowledge, in short, never in this way or anything at all like it." I am grateful to Nigel Thorp of the Centre for Whistler Studies, Hunterian Art Gallery, University of Glasgow, for pointing out this information to me.

3 With some Italian methods, the surface of the gilded frame is often painted over with a colored egg-tempera technique called "sgraffito." The paint is then scratched off with a wooden stylus, creating intricate linear designs that reveal a thin line of the underlying gold. In Kuehne's style of sgraffito, the artist omits the tempera layer, and scratches directly through the silver leaf with a metal tool to expose the gesso, resulting in a white line around the floral design.

4 "During 1914 Kuehne visited Spain for the first time, and he immediately fell under her spell. Here he remained three years. . . . He lived there long enough to absorb a great deal of Spanish atmosphere." A. E. Gallatin, *Max Kuehne* (New York: E. P. Dutton & Co, 1924), p. 6.

5 American Impressionist artists often commissioned artisans such as Frederick Harer, Bernard Badura, and Francis Coll to design and make frames. Harer was an artist and craftsman who created innovative and distinguished frames that were frequently adapted from Spanish and Italian patterns. His designs are basic freehand expressions that appear at once powerful and delicate. Harer's father was a cabinet maker who encouraged his son to attend the Pennsylvania Academy of the Fine Arts. The artist traveled to Europe and on his return in 1929, he began making frames in his Uhlerstown studio, "Red Cliff Studio" (possibly named after the famous Boston atelier, the Carrig-Rohane Shop—Irish for "Red Cliff"—later bought by Vose Galleries). He remarked to a reporter for *New Hope* magazine in 1933: "All my designs are based on fundamental truths that I hope will survive this period and all others, as the primitives have done. . . . I have spent as much as three months perfecting one piece. . . . there are a lot of people who appreciate individualism because its beauty will increase with time. . . ."

6 Cited in Ira Glackens, *William Glackens and the Ashcan Group* (New York: Crown Publishers Inc., 1957), p. 65.

7 Richard Kuehne (the artist's son), interview with the author, 1991. See also Max Kuehne's order book for Prendergast entry 1921–22. Kuehne was methodical and accurate about his accounts.

8 Silver leaf, white gold, and aluminum leaf can be covered with an orange-tinted varnish or shellac called "similoro," a mixture of gamboge and dragonsblood (two organic pigments), to impart a distinctive cool gold effect.

9 Kuehne experimented with various frame-finishing techniques until he arrived at a style that would not dominate his paintings. See Horace Wesley Ott, "Max Kuehne's Furniture in Gesso," *International Studio* 84 (July 1926), pp. 71–75.

10 Frames made by Kuehne appear on *Madonna and Child*, Italian (Byzantine), 14th century, in the collection of the Rochester Memorial Art Gallery, N. Y.; and *Dancer Adjusting Her Bodice*, c. 1889, by Edgar Degas, in the collection of the Art Institute of Chicago.

PLATES

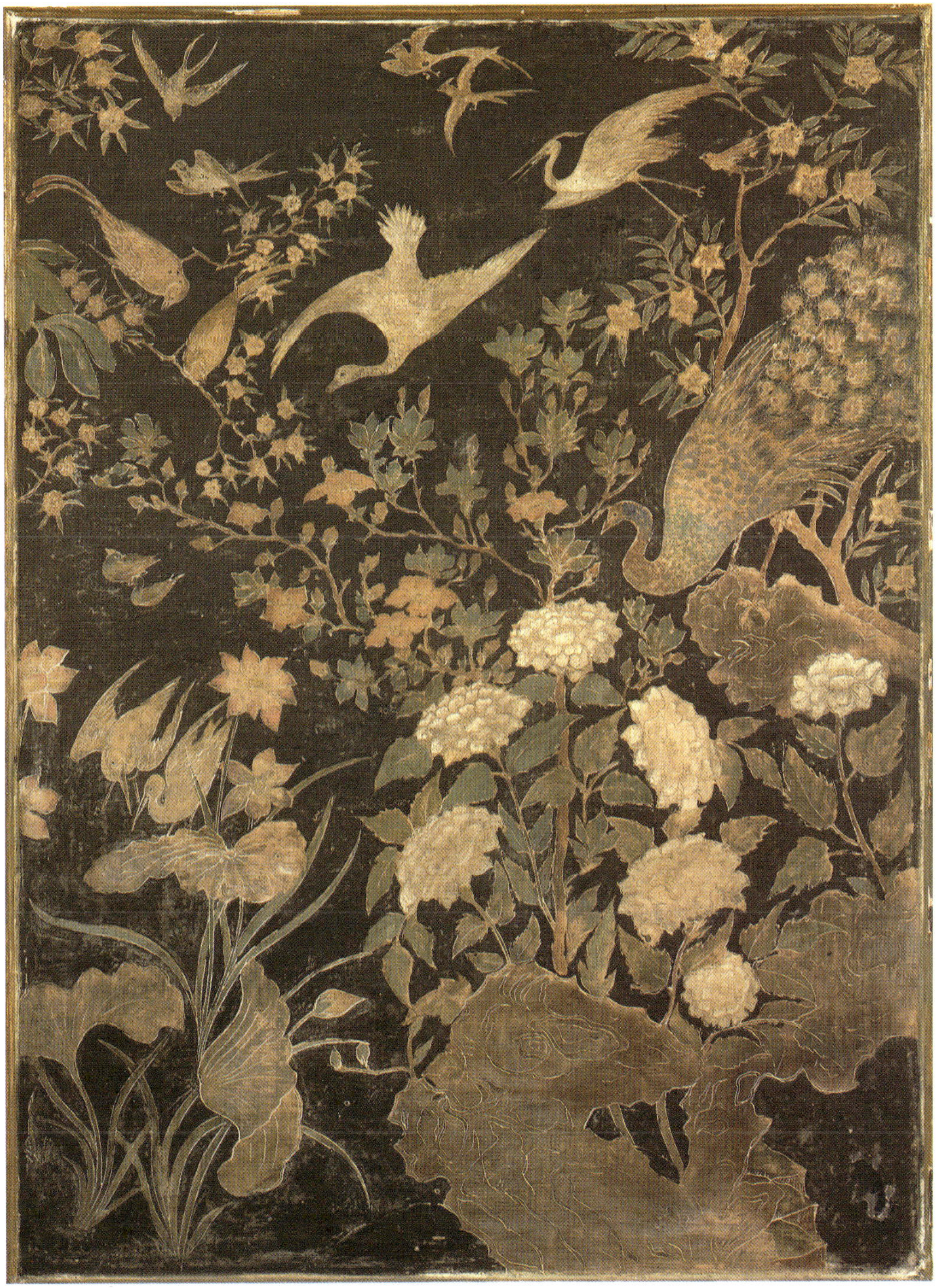

1
Decorative incised panel
(Peacock and Egrets), c. 1950
Gessoed wood, watercolor, silver leaf, shellac
48 × 36 × 1 inches
Collection of Ann M. Beal

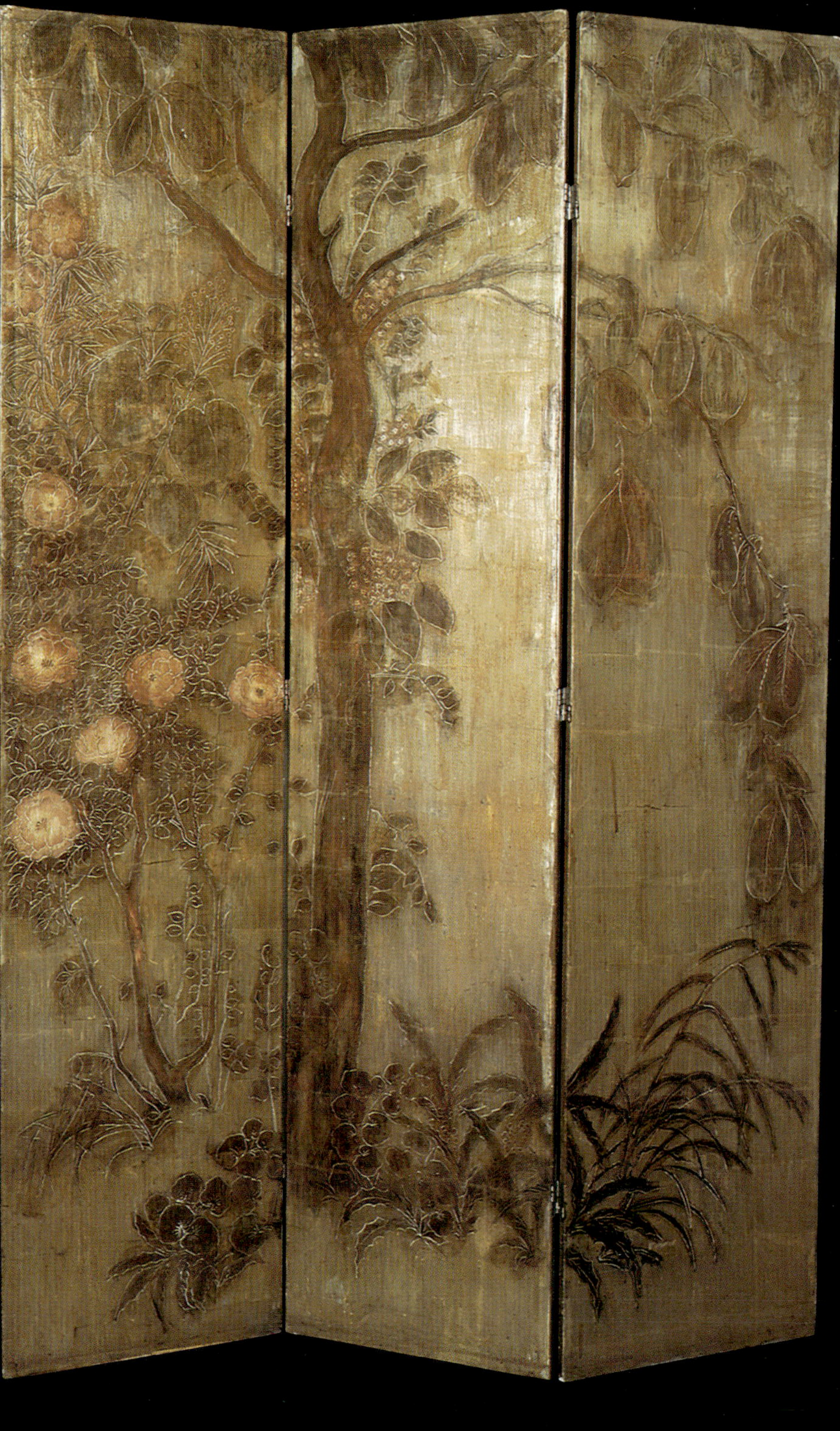

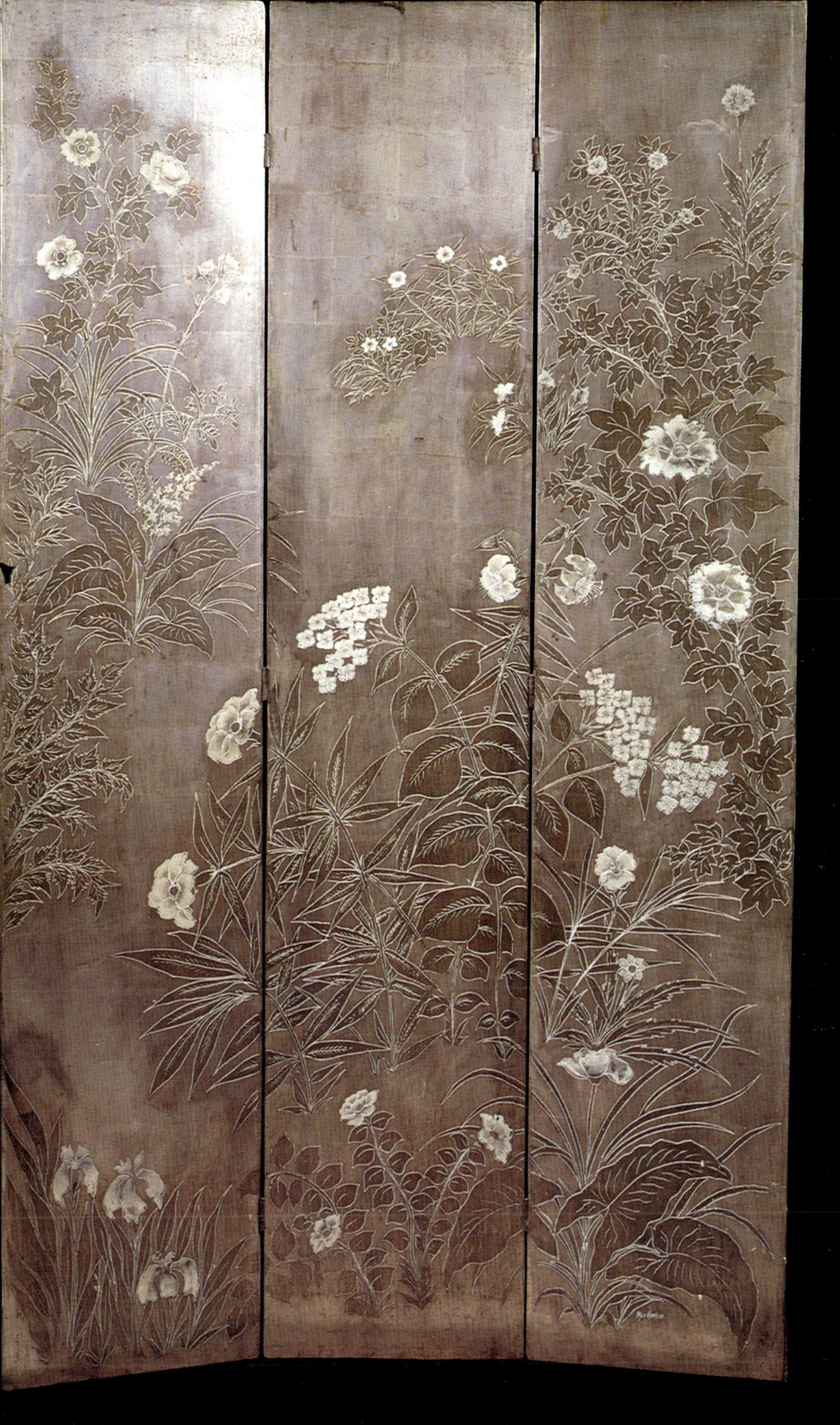

3
Three-paneled folding screen *(White Flowers and Foliage)*, c. 19
Gessoed wood, watercolor, silver leaf, shellac
72¾ × 43½ × ¾ inches
Incised bottom center on right panel: "Max Kuehne"
Displayed framed in exhibition.

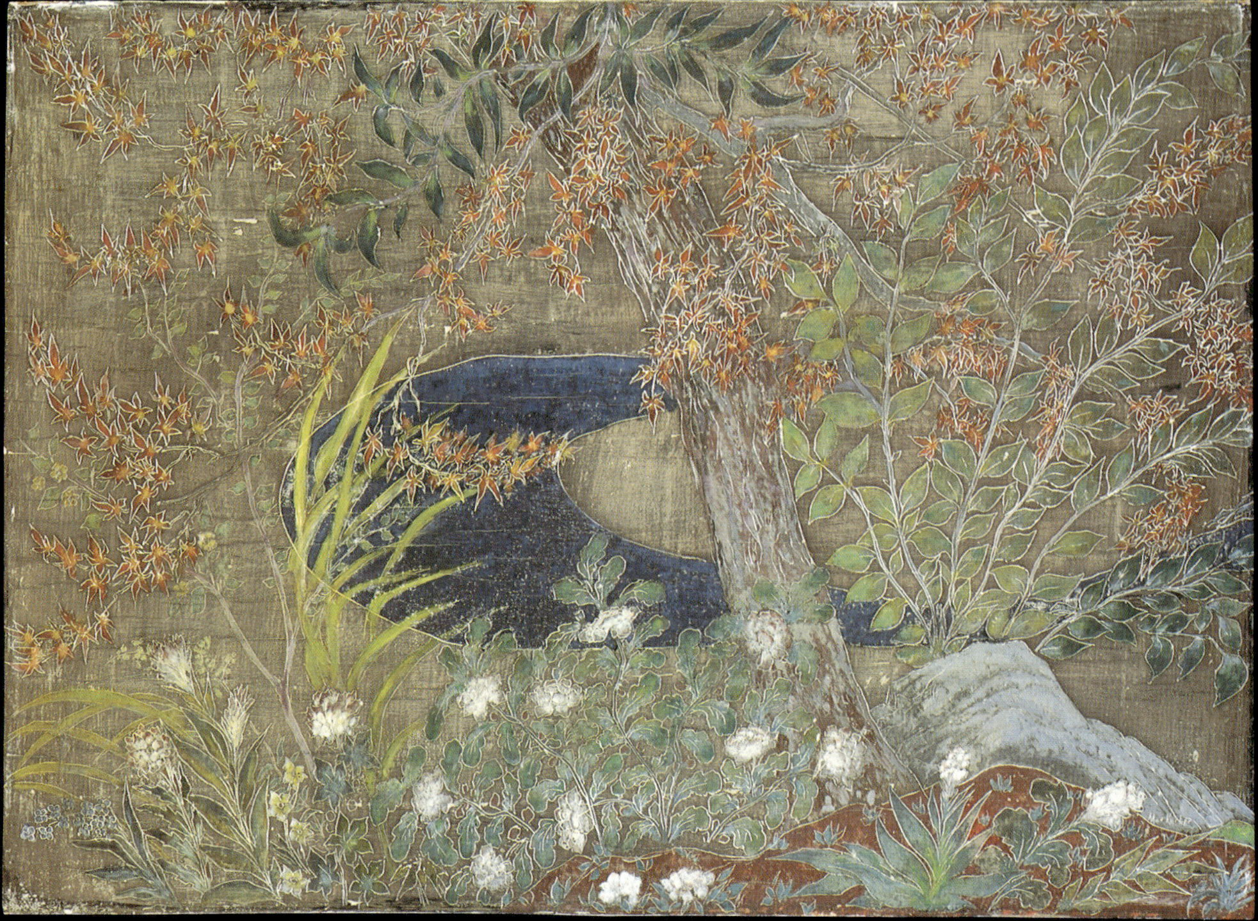

4
Framed decorative incised panel *(Tree of Life)*, late 1920s
Gessoed panel, watercolor, silver leaf
28 × 39 inches
Incised lower right: "M. Kuehne"
Private collection

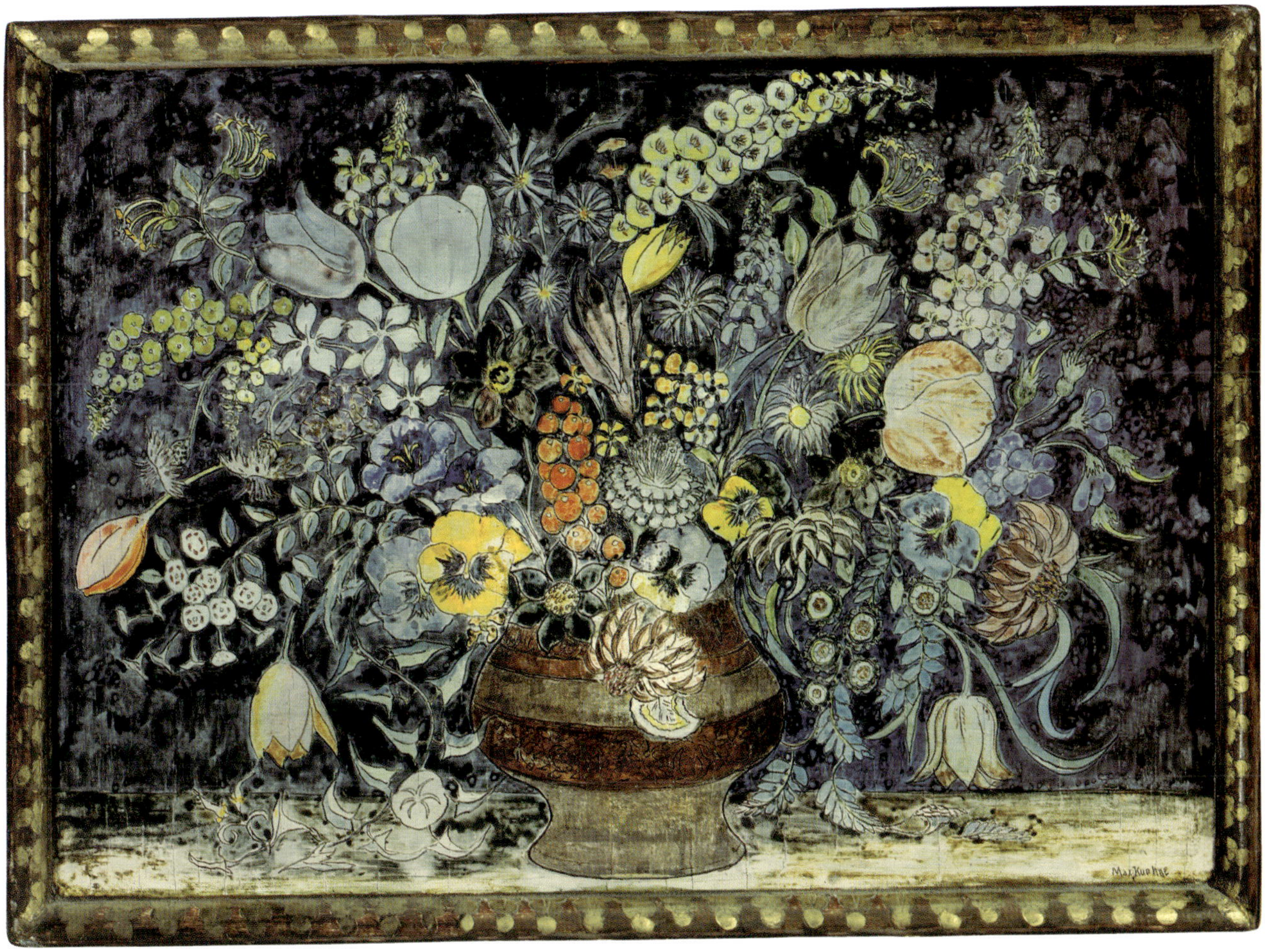

5
Tray *(Still Life with Flowers and Berries)*, c. 1925–28
Gessoed wood, watercolor, silver leaf, shellac
$20\frac{1}{2} \times 29 \times 1\frac{1}{8}$ inches
Incised lower right: "Max Kuehne"

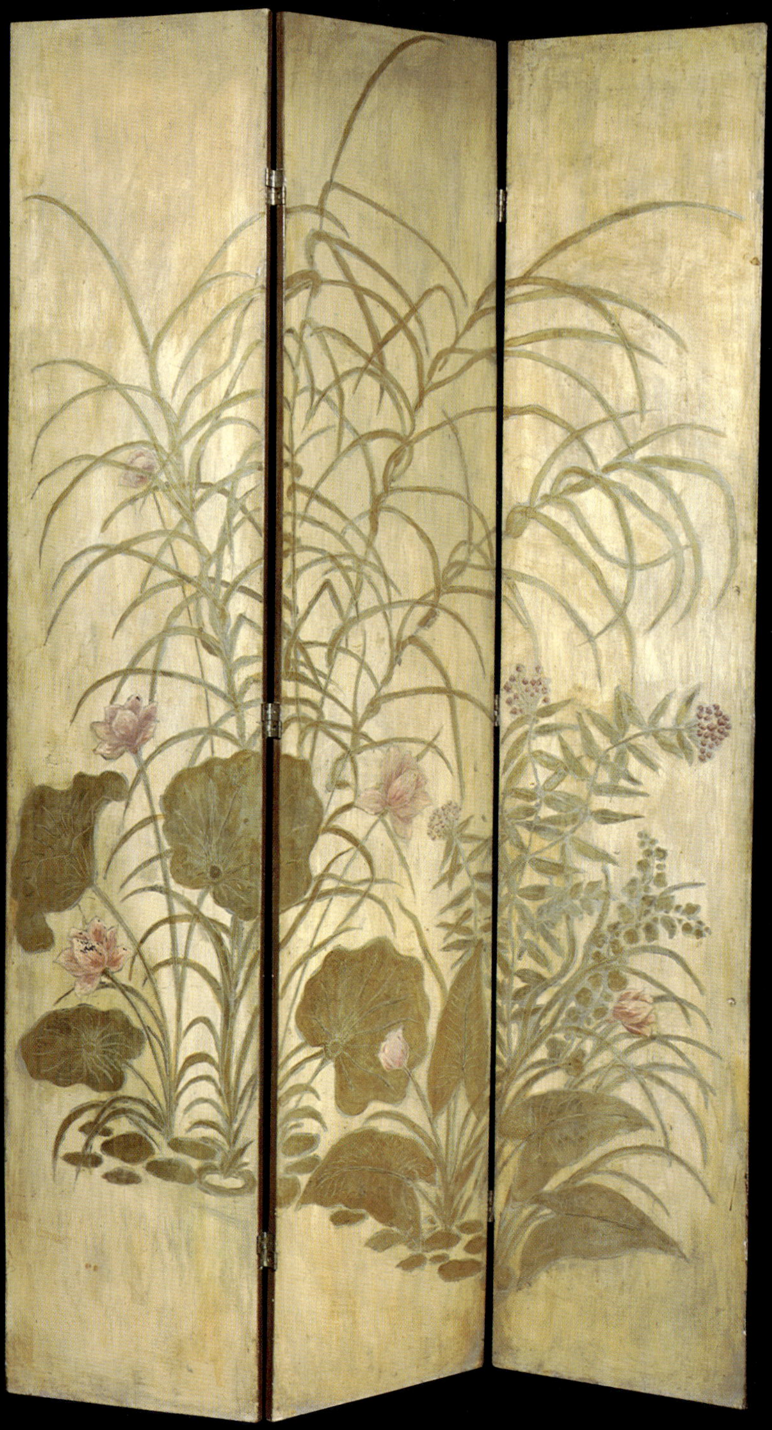

verso

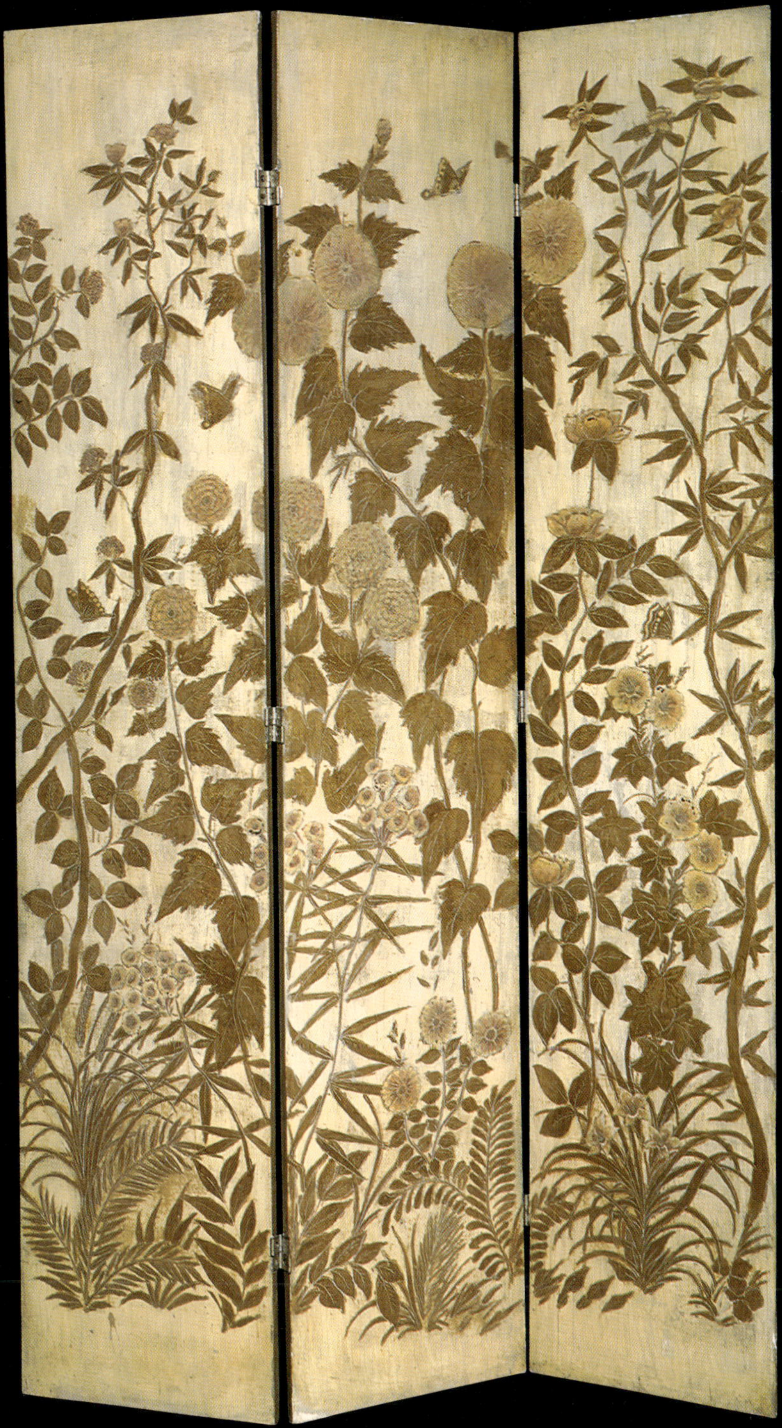

recto

6

Double-sided three-paneled folding screen *(Leaves and Grasses)*, c. 1930s–40s
Gessoed wood, watercolor, silver leaf, shellac
$72 \times 45\frac{3}{4} \times \frac{3}{4}$ inches
Inscribed lower right on recto: "Max Kuehne"

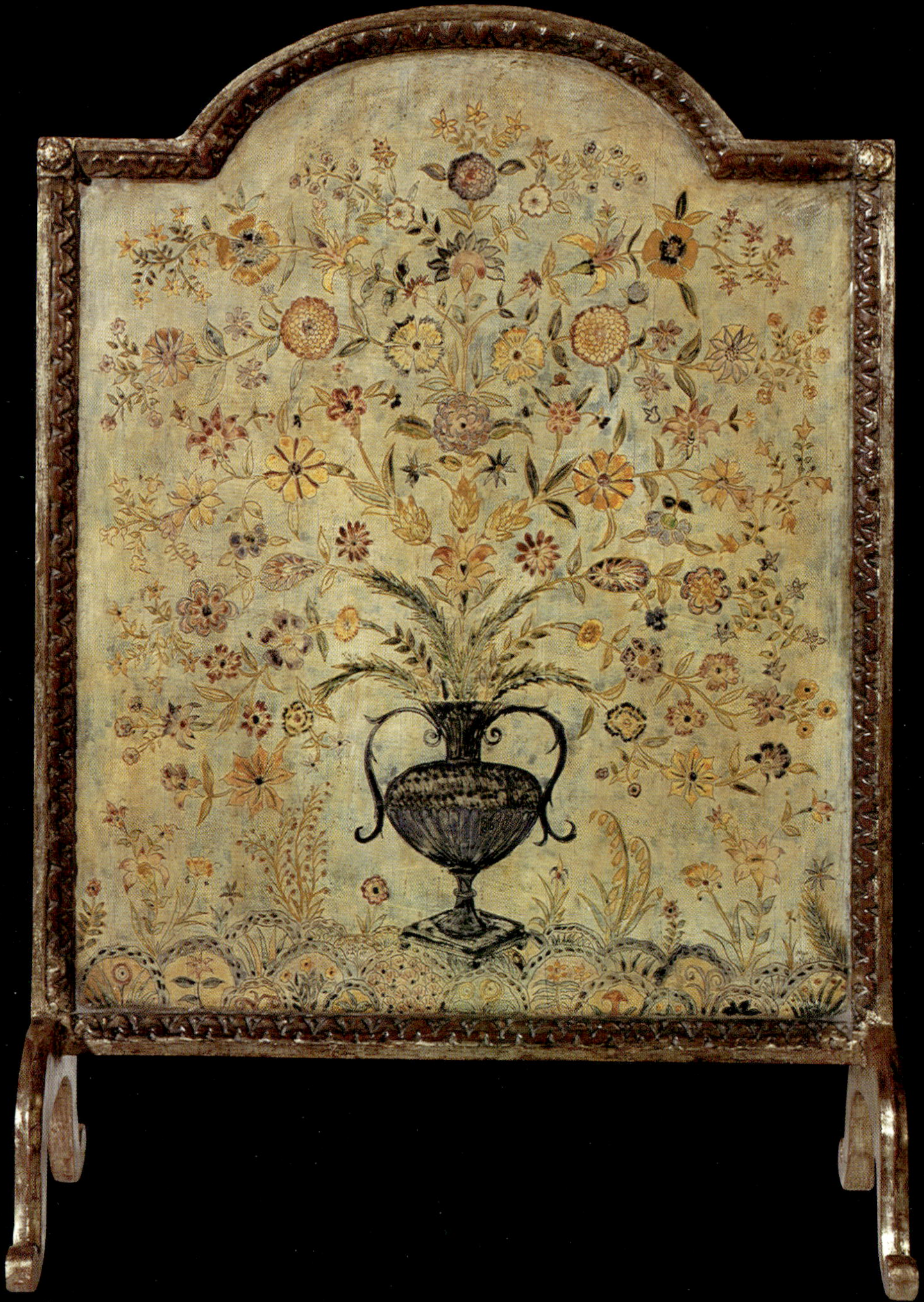

7
Double-sided fire screen *(Flowers in Black Urn)*, recto, c. 1925–35
Gessoed wood, watercolor, silver leaf, shellac
36 × 26 inches
Signed lower right: "Max Kuehne"
Private collection, Jim's Antiques Fine Art Gallery, Lambertville, N. J.

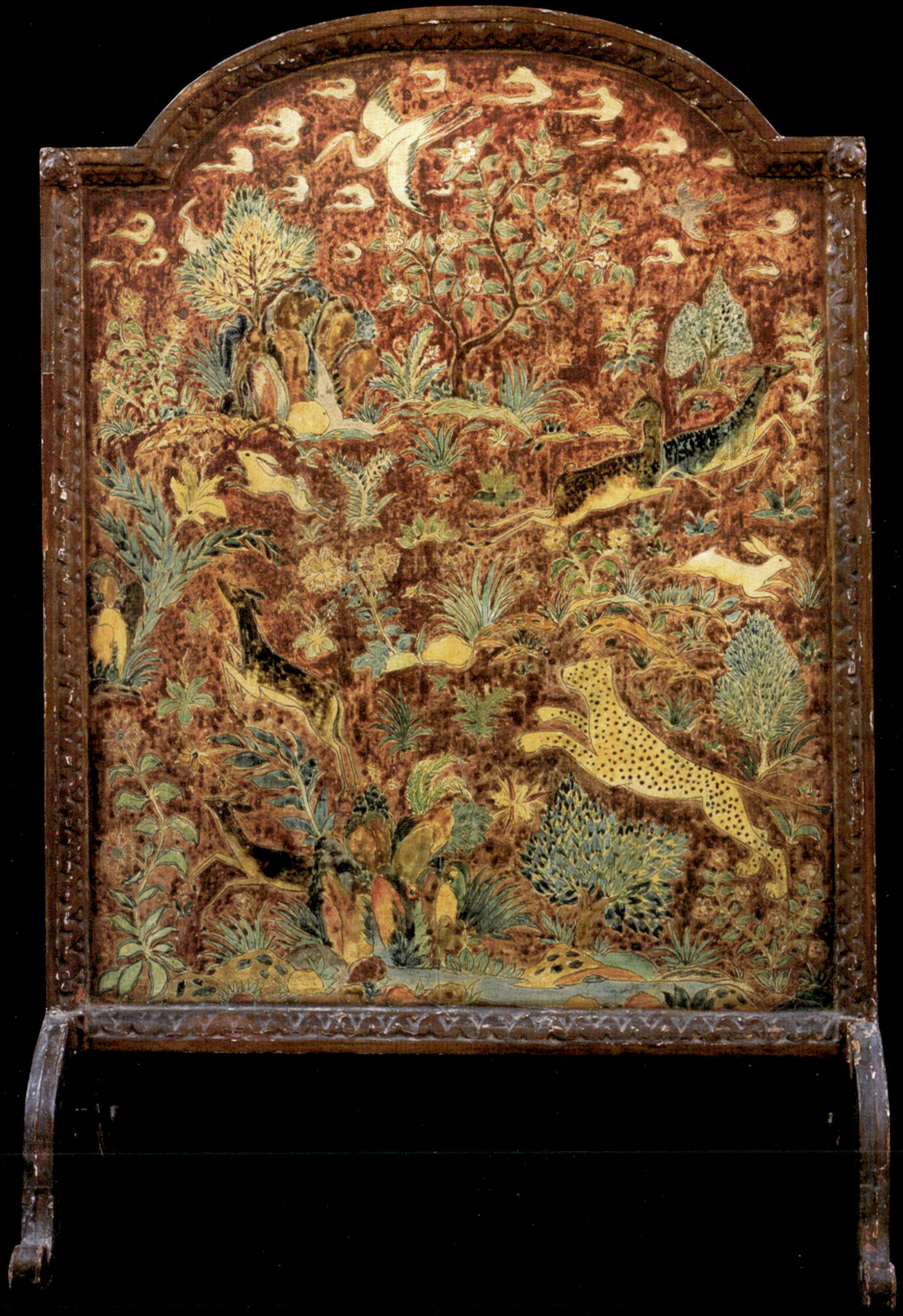

8
Fire screen *(Deer and Leopard in Landscape)*, c. 1930s
Gessoed wood, watercolor, silver leaf, shellac
36 × 25 × 11½ inches
Collection of Ann M. Beal

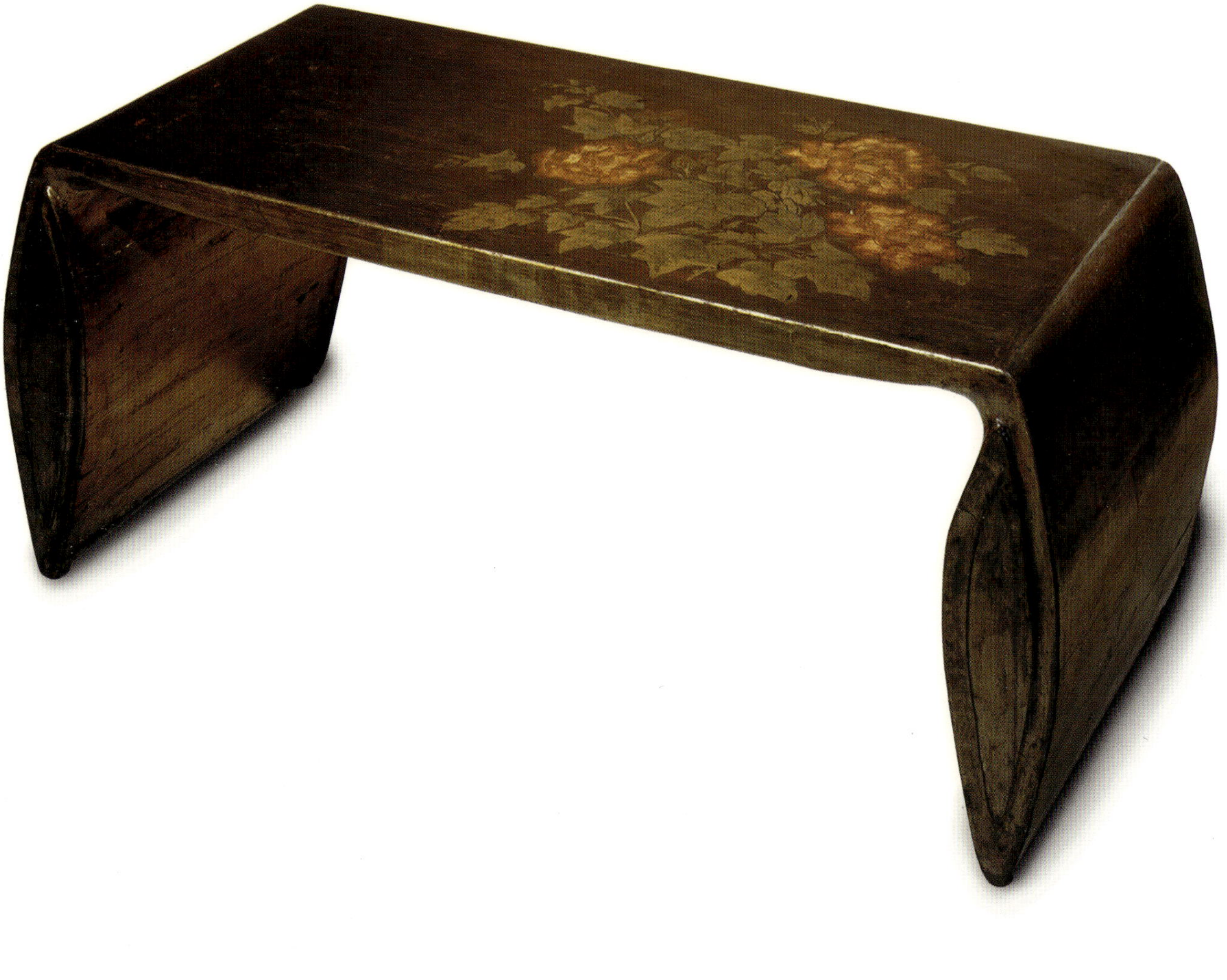

9
Cocktail table *(Cluster of Copper Flowers)*, c. 1940s
Gessoed wood, watercolor, silver leaf, lacquer
16½ × 41 × 18 inches
Incised lower right: "Max Kuehne"

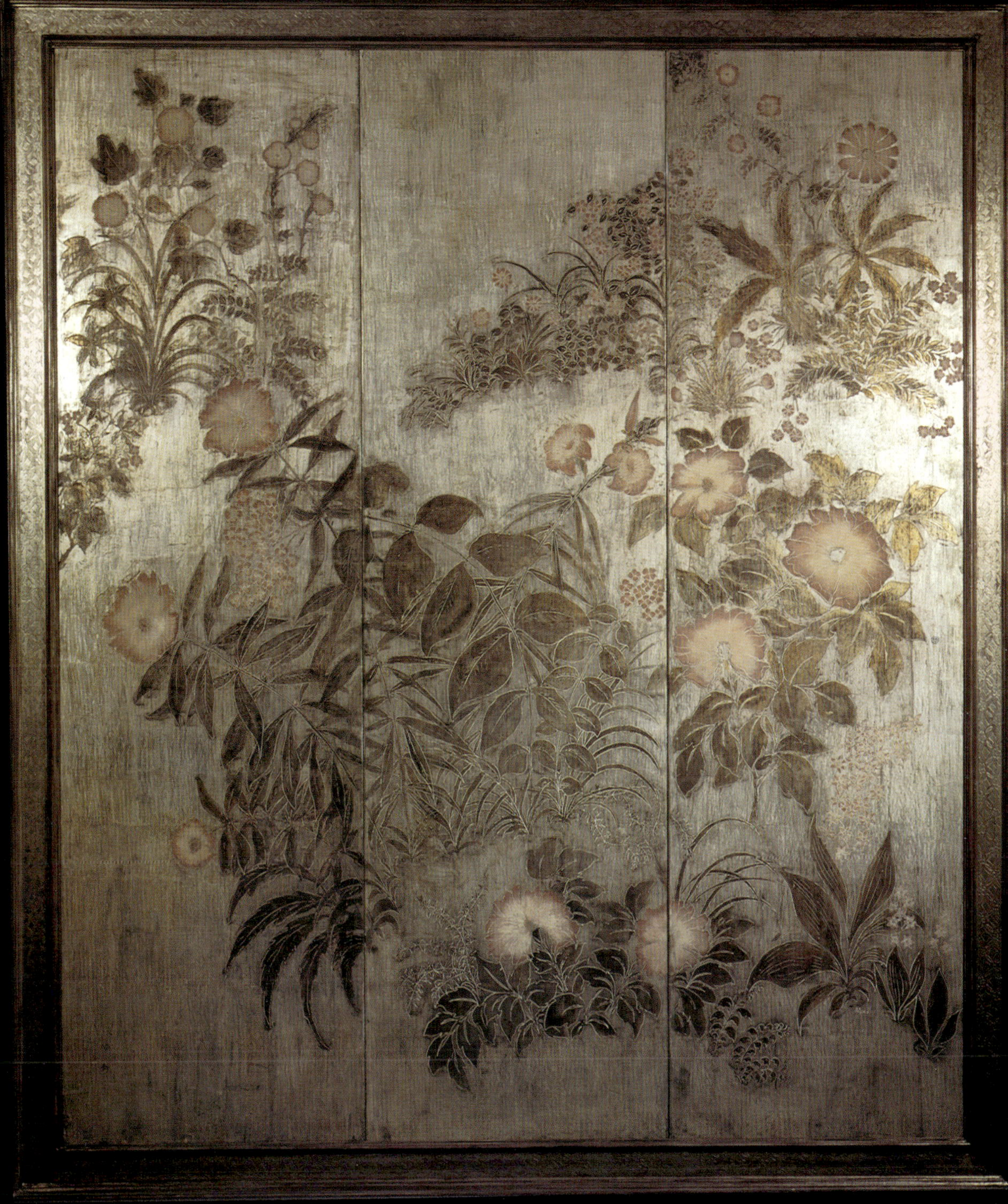

10

Framed three-paneled screen *(Floral Arrangement in Pink and Silver)*, c. 1930s–40s
Gessoed wood, watercolor, silver leaf, shellac
83½ × 71½ × ¾ inches
Incised lower right: "Max Kuehne"

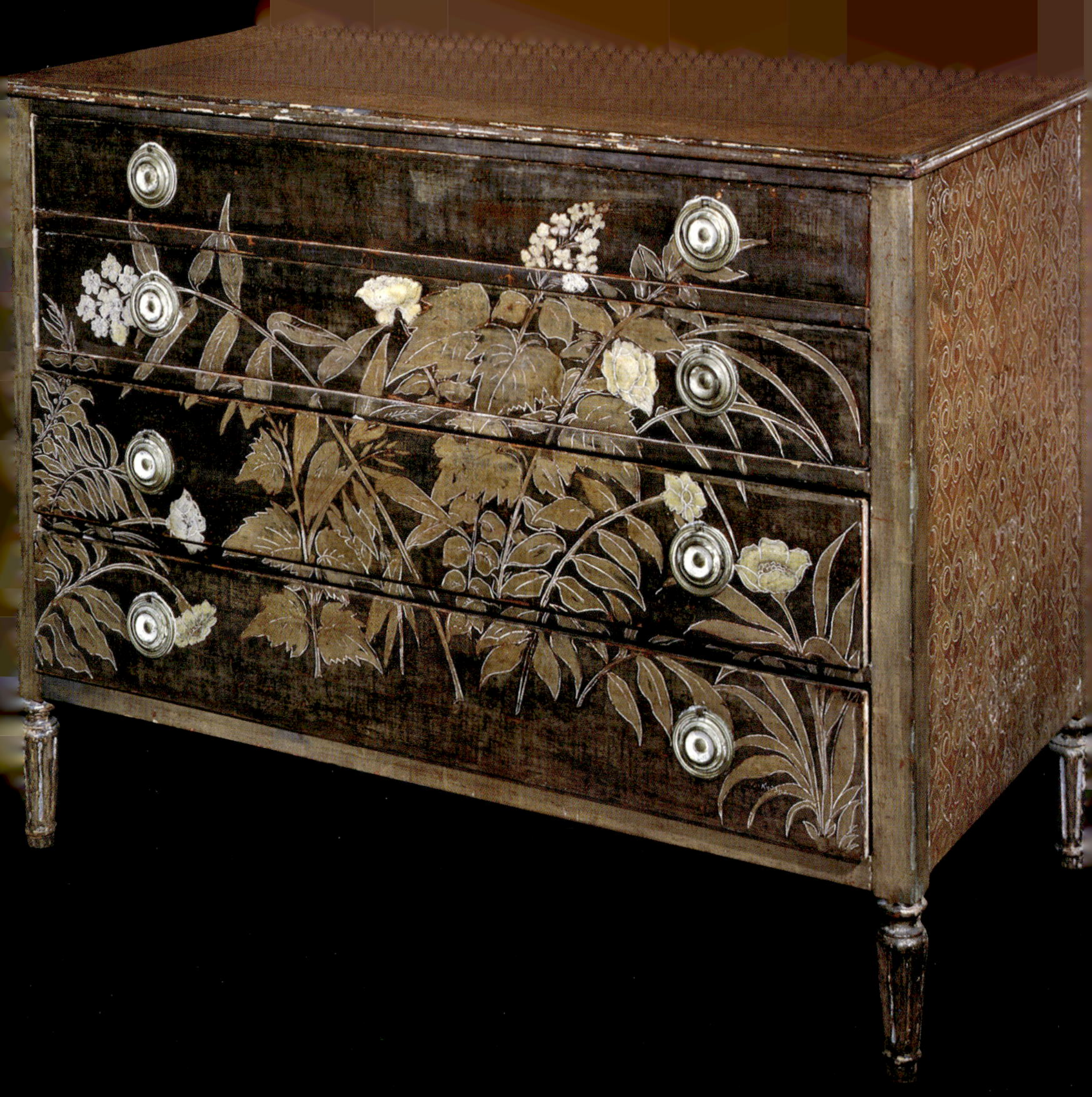

11

Chest of drawers on legs *(Ferns and Flowers)*, c. 1950–60s
Four drawers with circular metal pulls
Gessoed wood, watercolor, silver leaf, lacquer
33½ × 43 × 22½ inches
Incised lower right on bottom drawer: "Max Kuehne"

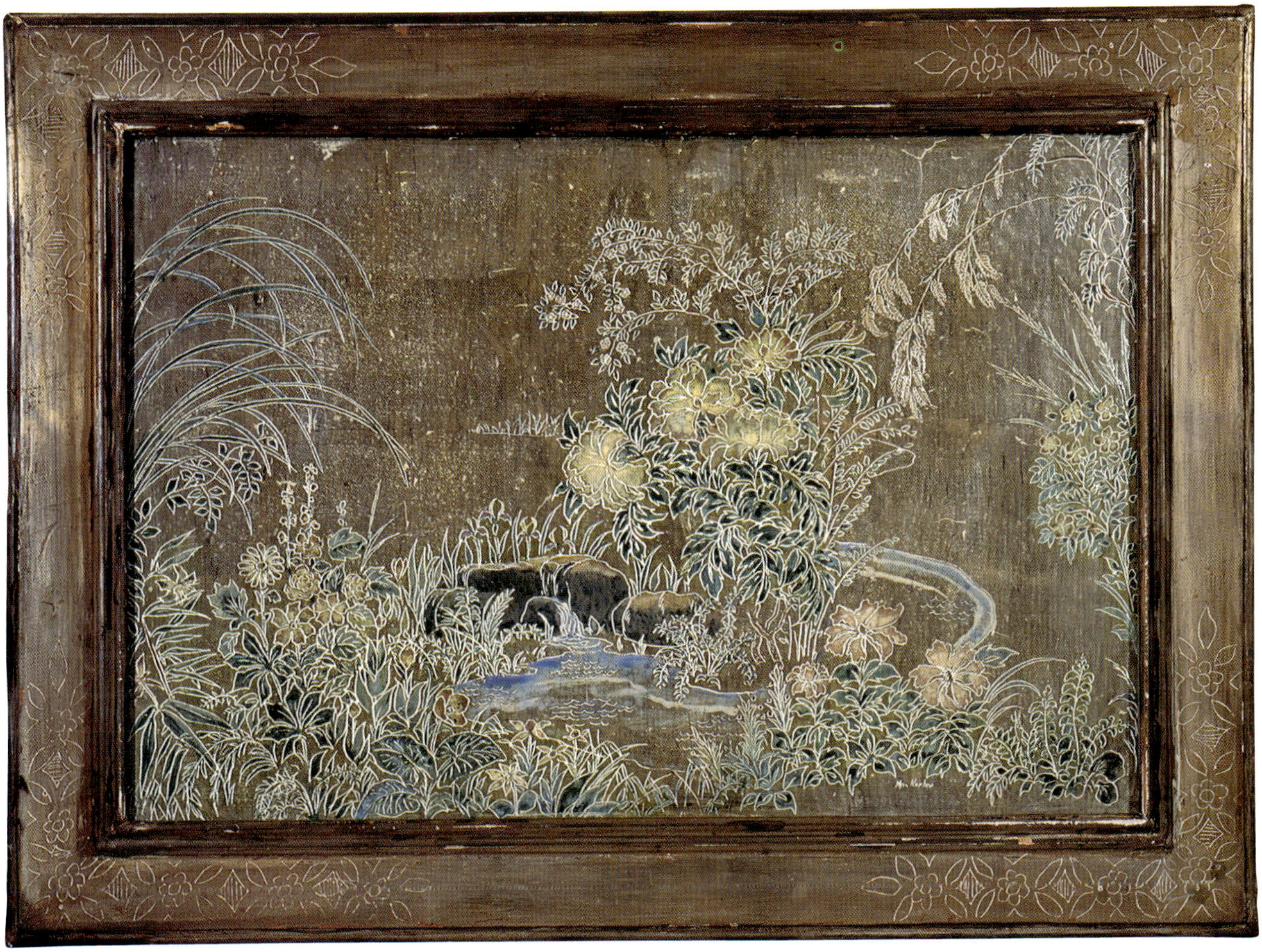

12
Framed decorative incised panel
(Edge of the Cove), c. 1930s
Gessoed panel, watercolor, silver leaf, shellac
19¼ × 29⅛ inches
Incised lower right: "Max Kuehne"
Frame by Max Kuehne

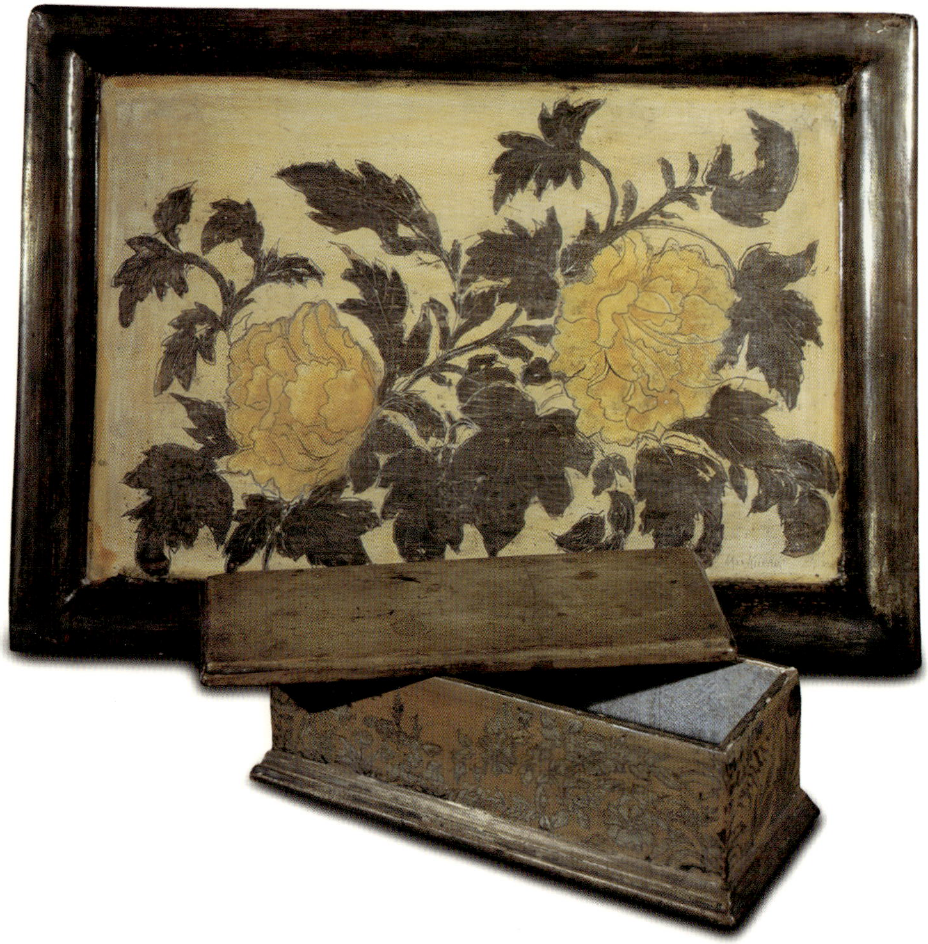

13
Tray *(Yellow Peonies)*, c. 1930s
Gessoed wood, watercolor, silver leaf, lacquer
13¼ × 19 × 1⅛ inches
Incised lower right: "Max Kuehne"
Courtesy of Avis Berman

14
Decorative box, c. 1930s
Gessoed panel, watercolor, silver leaf, shellac
4 × 10 × 3 inches
Courtesy of Avis Berman

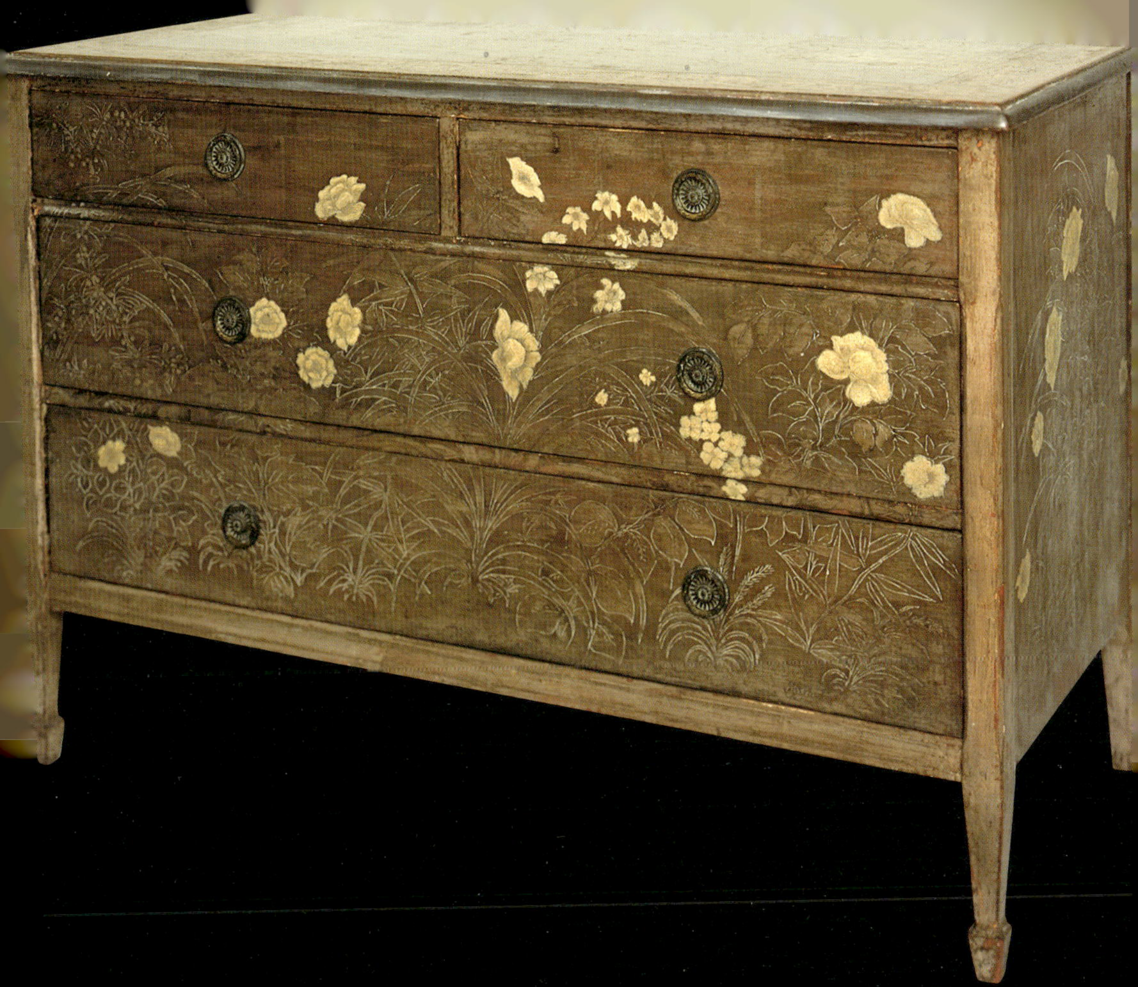

15
Chest of drawers on arrow-toed legs *(Floral Spray)*, c. 1950–60s
Four drawers with circular metal pulls
Gessoed wood, watercolor, silver leaf, lacquer
49¾ × 33¼ × 23 inches
Incised lower right on bottom drawer: “Max Kuehne”

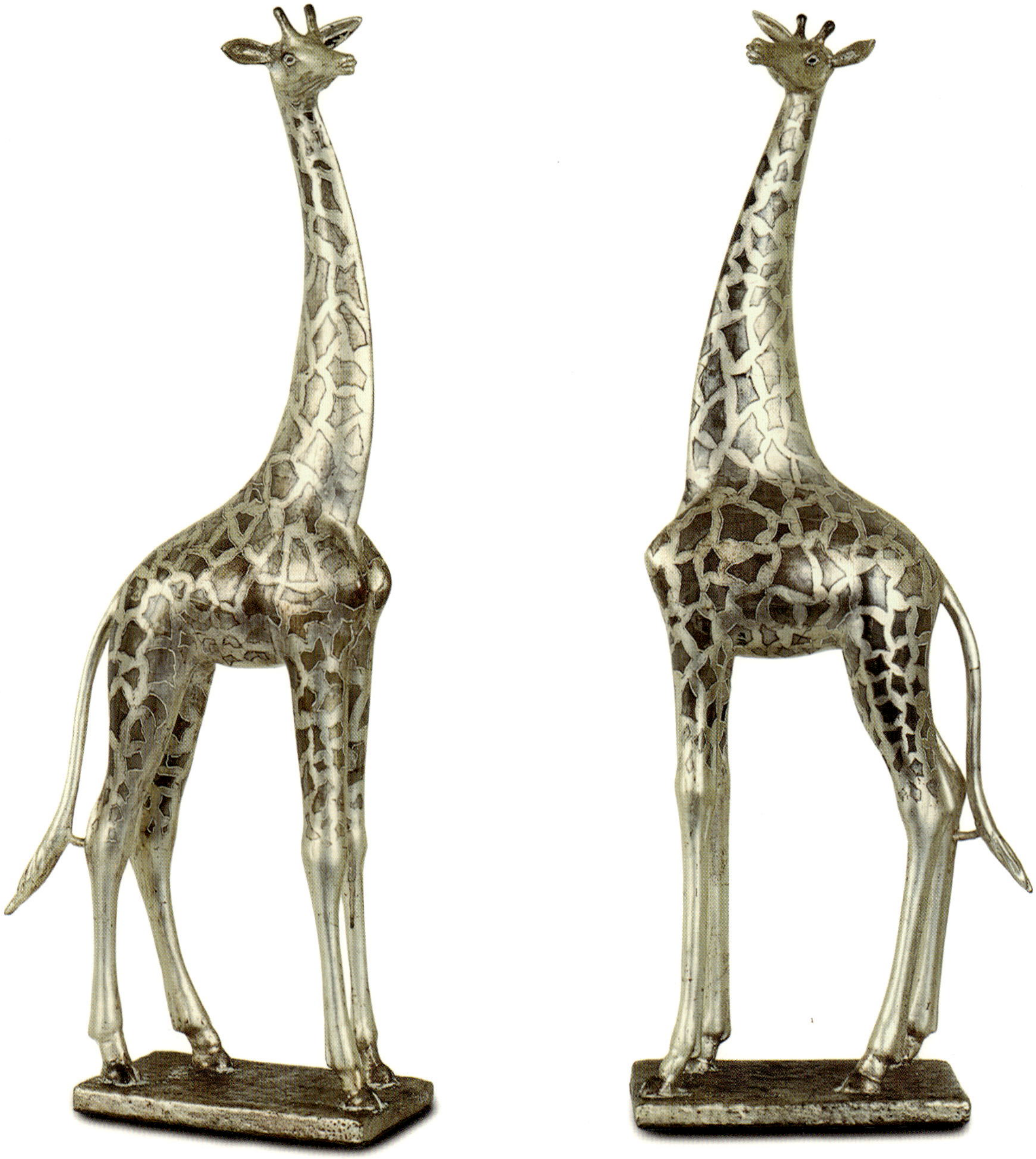

16
(Pair of Giraffes), c. 1940,
restored c. 1970 by Richard Kuehne
Gessoed wood and silver leaf
35¼ × 14 inches
Signed on base: "Max/Richard Kuehne"
Collection of Mr. and Mrs. Richard Kuehne

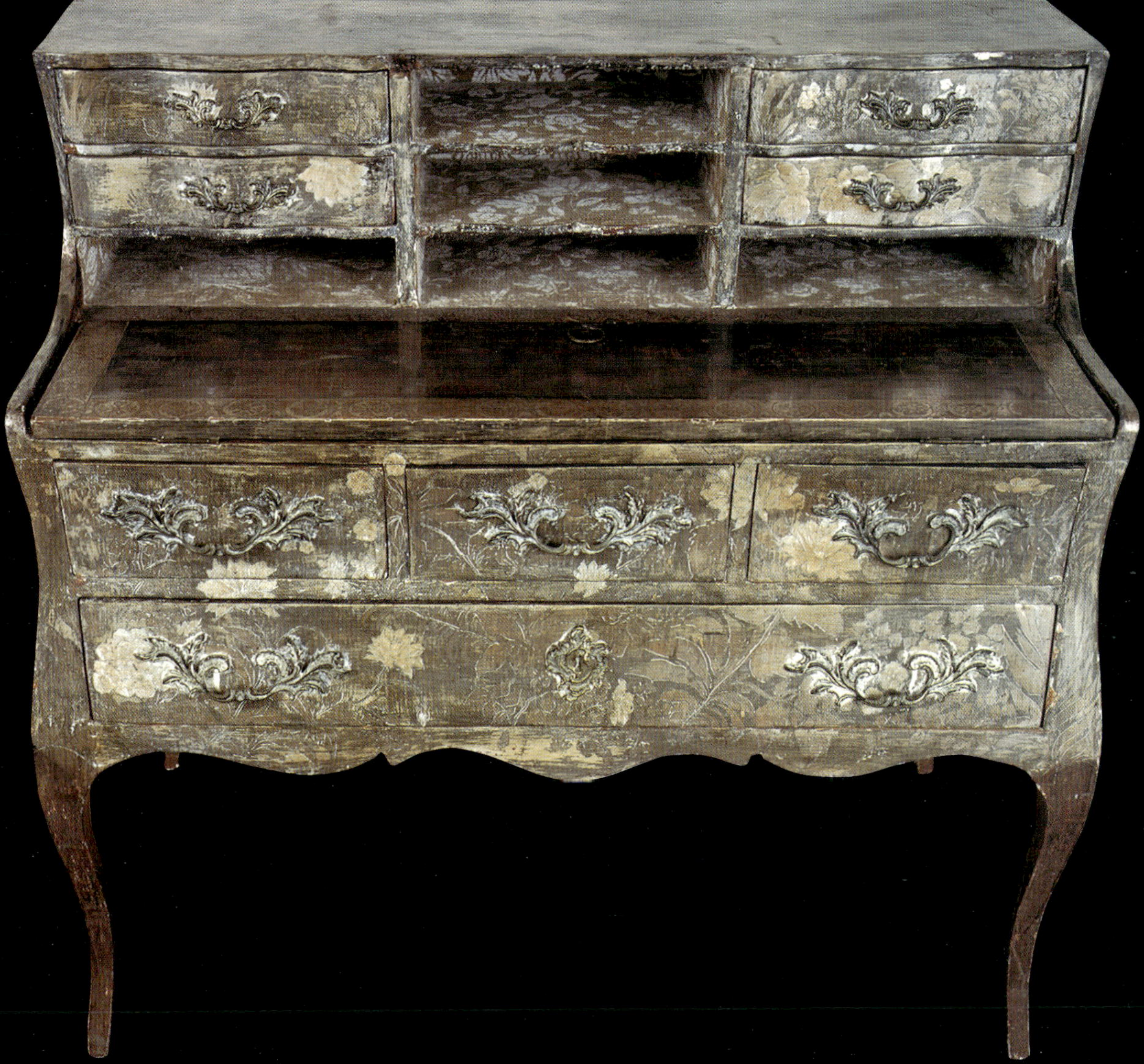

17

Secretary with tapering legs *(Continuous Patterning of Flowers and Leaves)*, c. 1964
Eight drawers with metal fleurs-de-lis pulls
Gessoed wood, watercolor, silver leaf, lacquer
39 × 42½ × 23 inches
Collection of Mr. and Mrs. Richard Kuehne

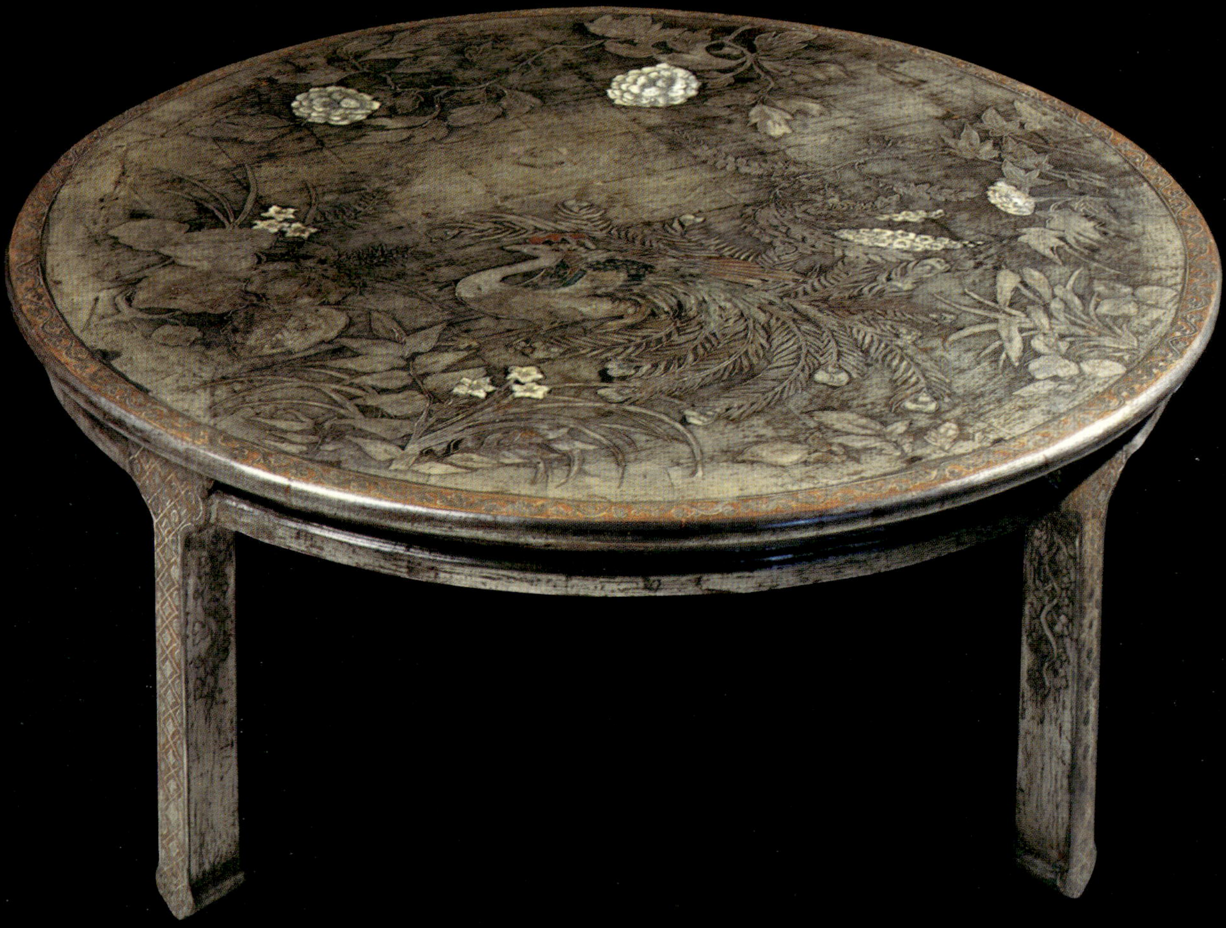

18
Round table *(Peacock and Foliage)*, c. 1930s
Gessoed wood, watercolor, silver leaf, lacquer
15⅛ × 39¼ inches
Incised center right: "Max Kuehne"
Baker/Pisano Collection

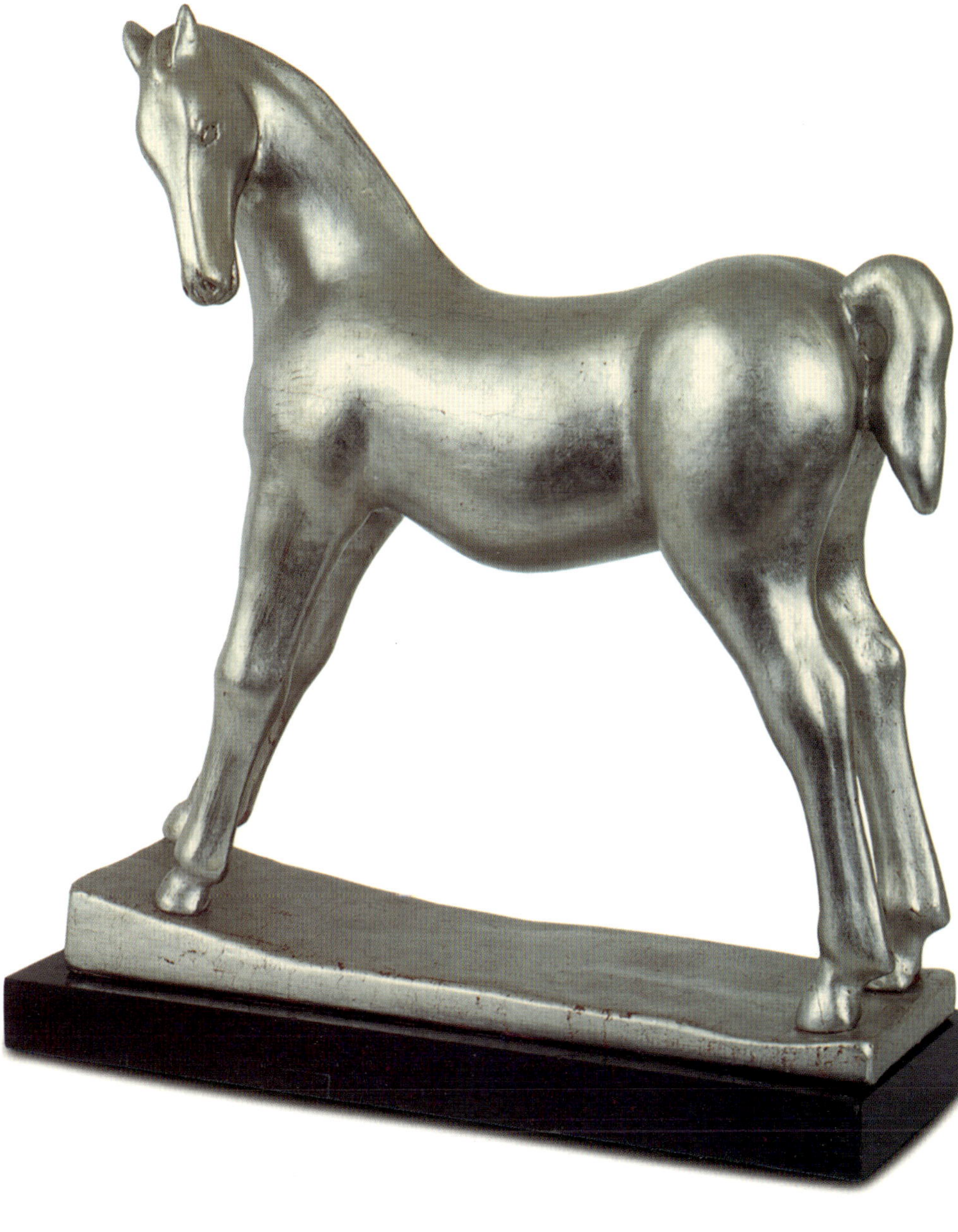

19
(Horse), c. 1930
Gessoed wood and palladium leaf on black marble base
17¼ × 12½ × 4 inches
Collection of Mr. and Mrs. Richard Kuehne

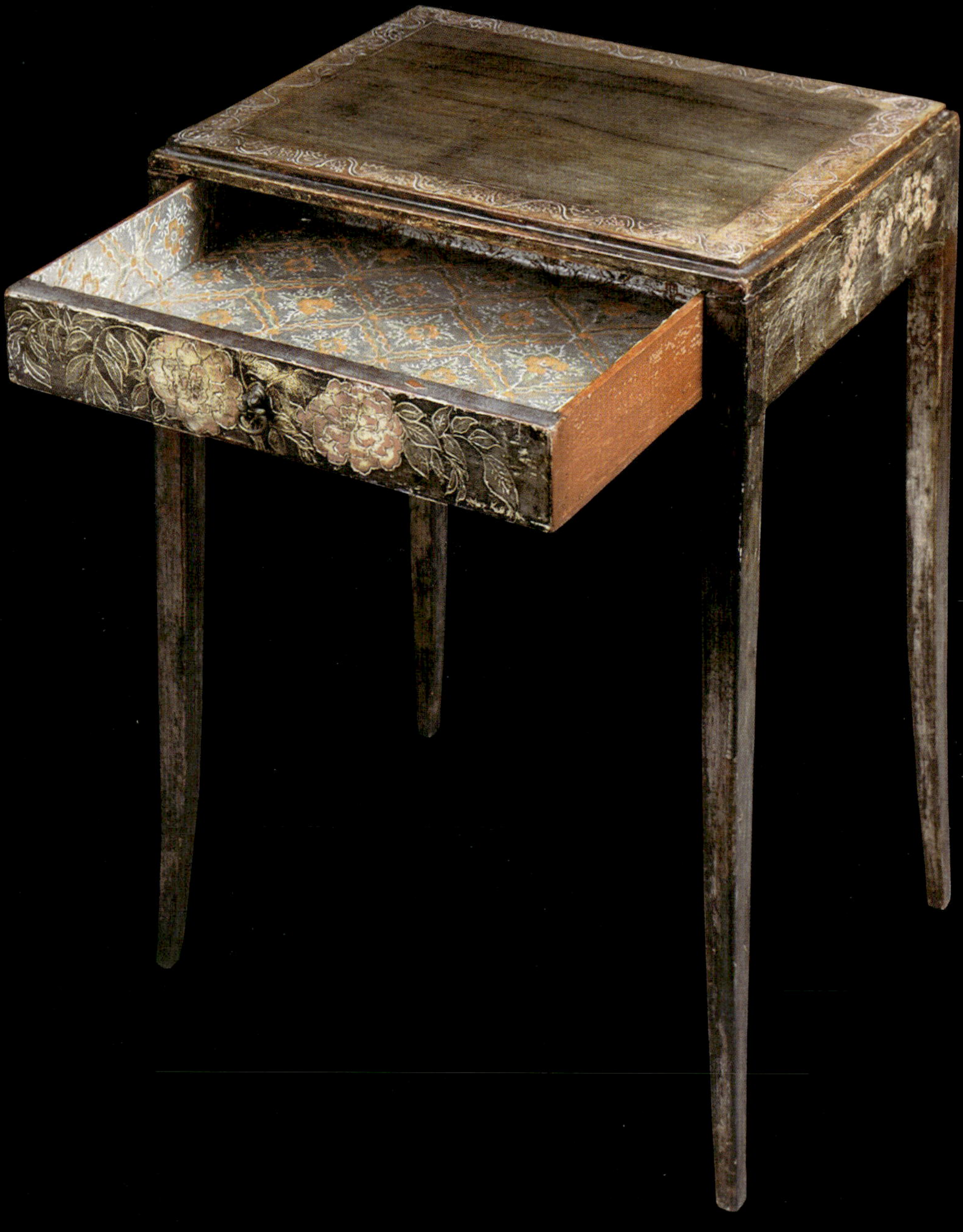

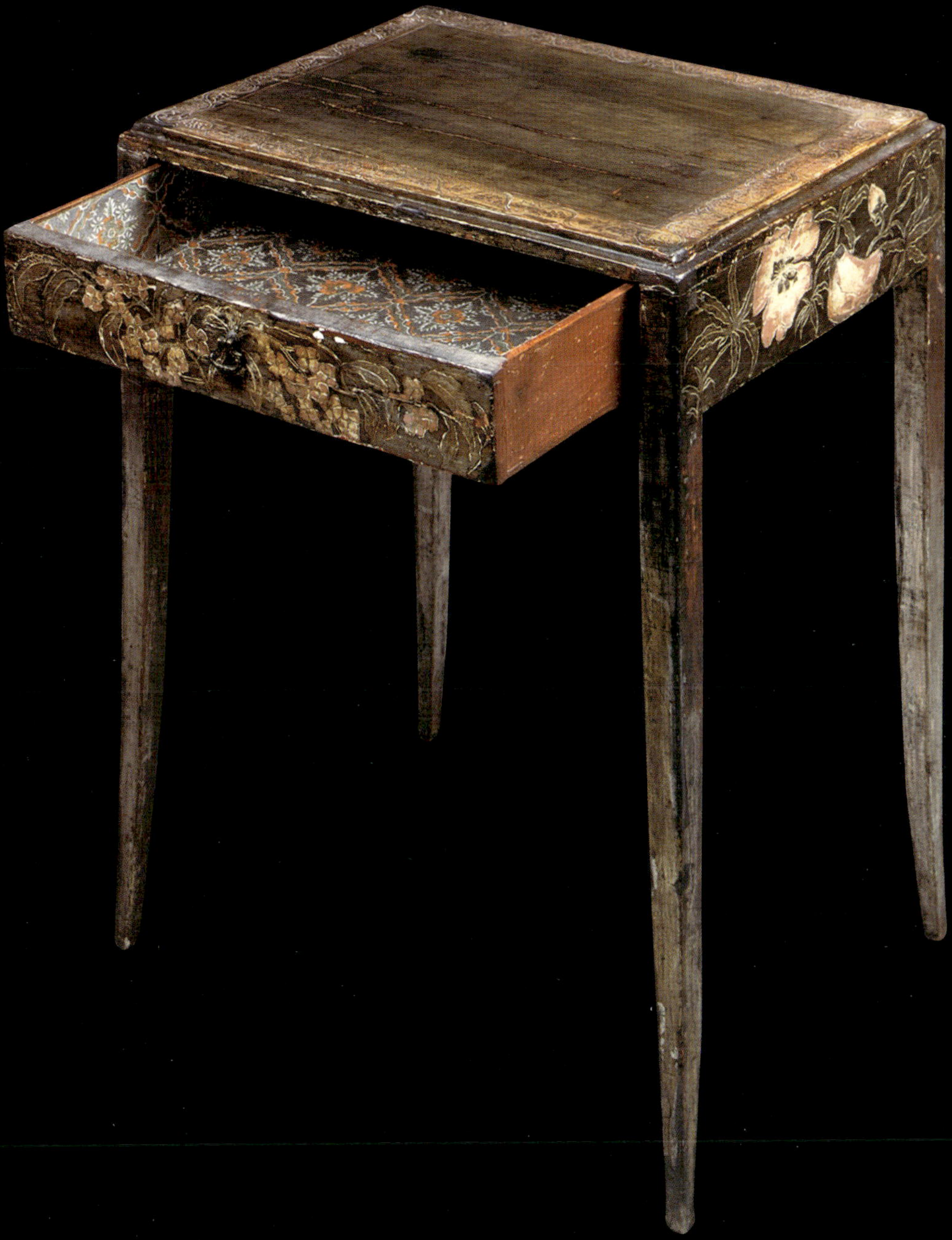

20
Pair of end tables *(Floral Frieze)*, c. 1950s
Each with a single drawer lined with Chinese wallpaper
Gessoed wood, watercolor, silver leaf, lacquer
25⅝ × 19 × 14½ inches each
Incised lower right on each drawer: "Max Kuehne"

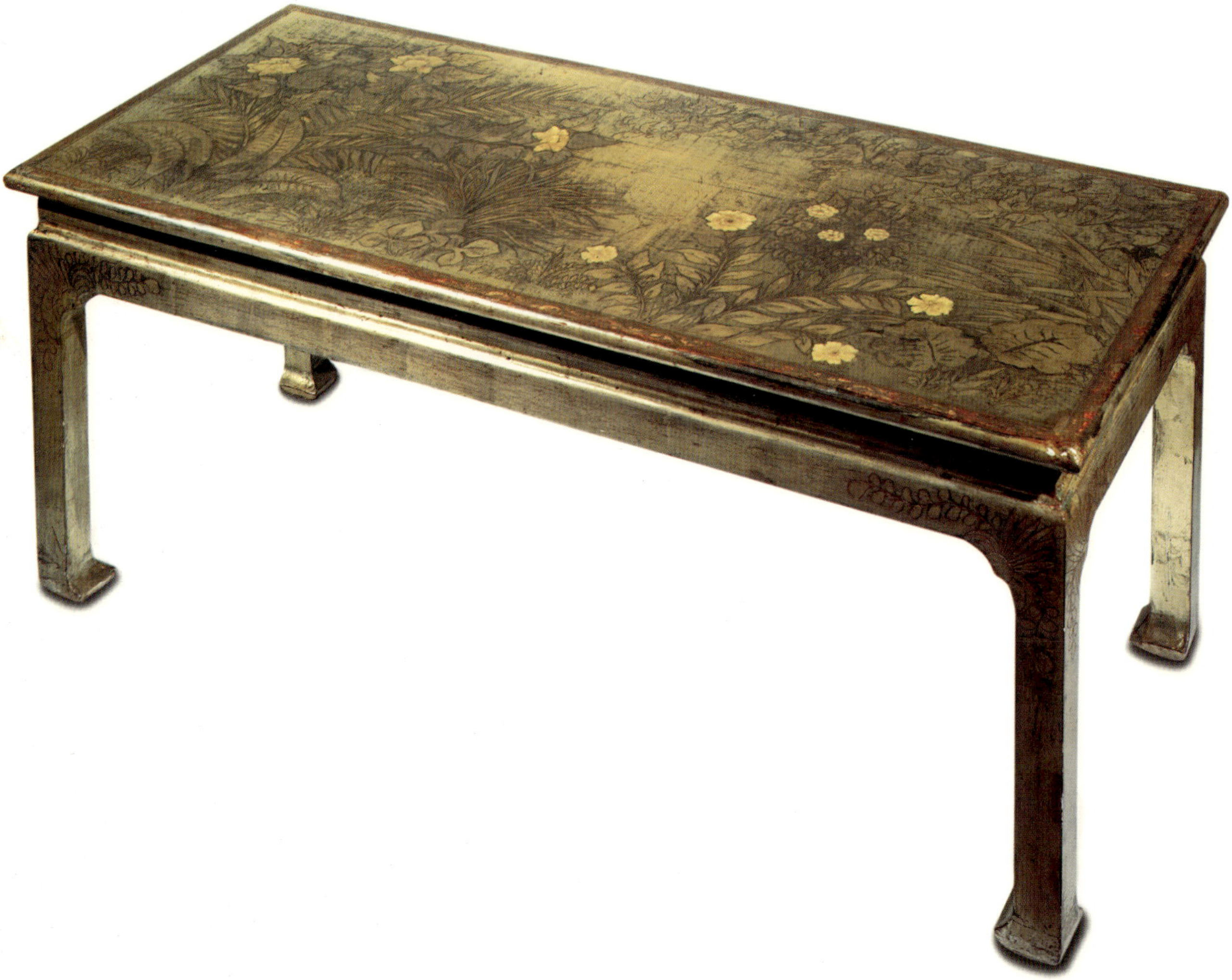

21
Cocktail table *(Primroses)*, c. 1930s–40s
Gessoed wood, watercolor, silver leaf, lacquer
16½ × 42 × 18⅜ inches
Incised lower right: "Max Kuehne"

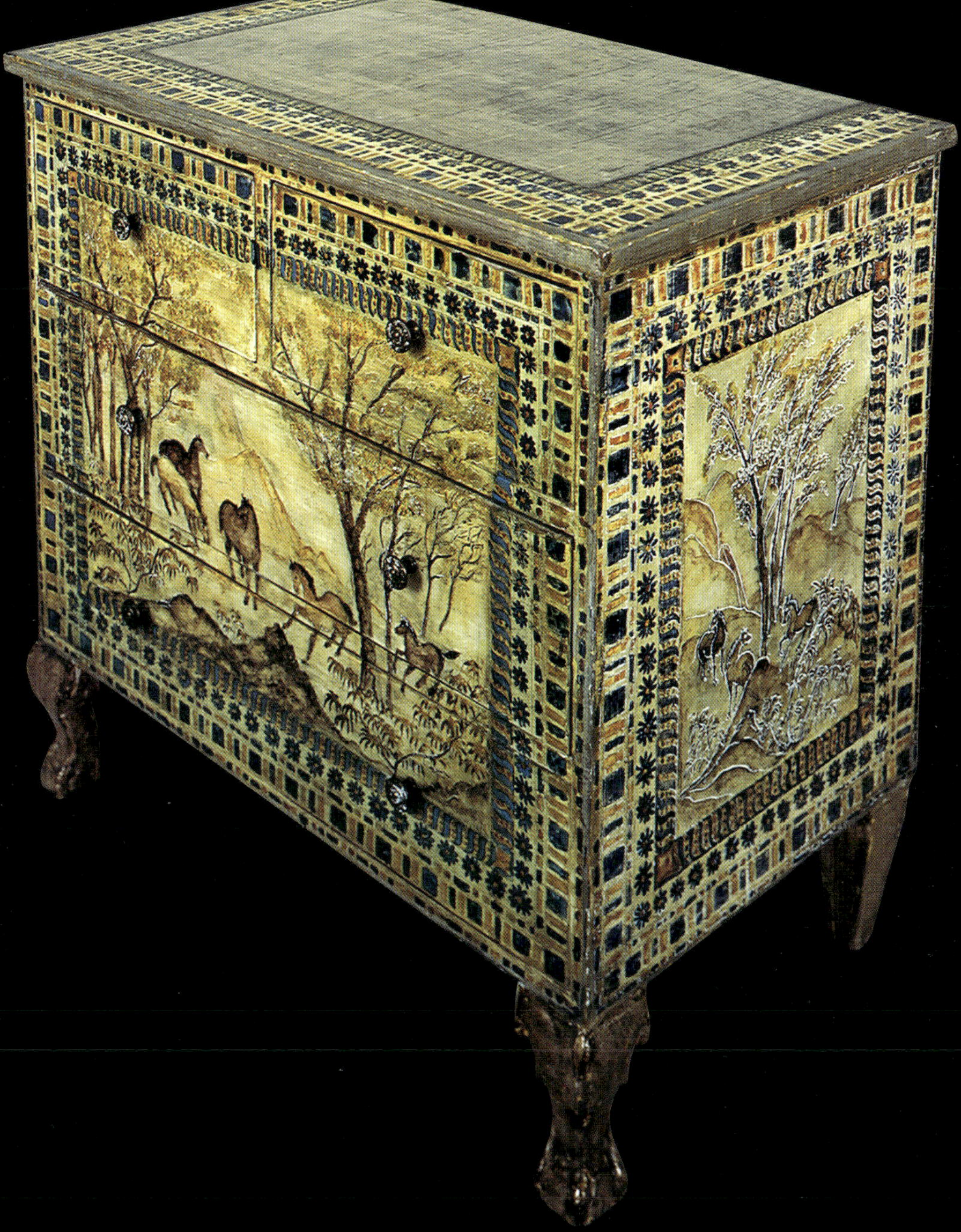

22

Chest *(Horses in a Landscape)*, c. 1930s
Four drawers lined with Chinese wallpaper, metal knobs as pulls
Gessoed wood, watercolor, silver leaf, shellac
29½ × 31 × 18¼ inches
Signed on lower bottom drawer: "Max Kuehne"
Collection of Mr. and Mrs. Richard Kuehne

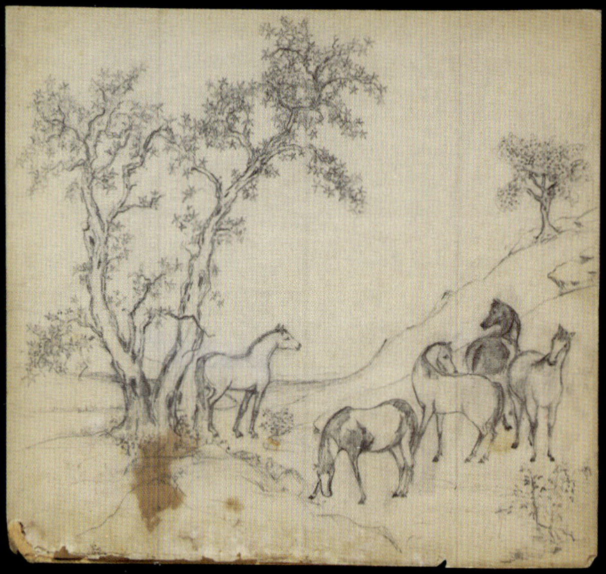

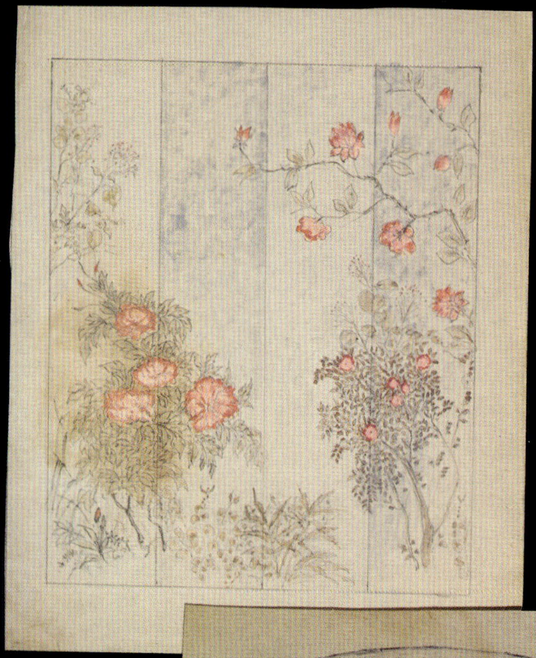

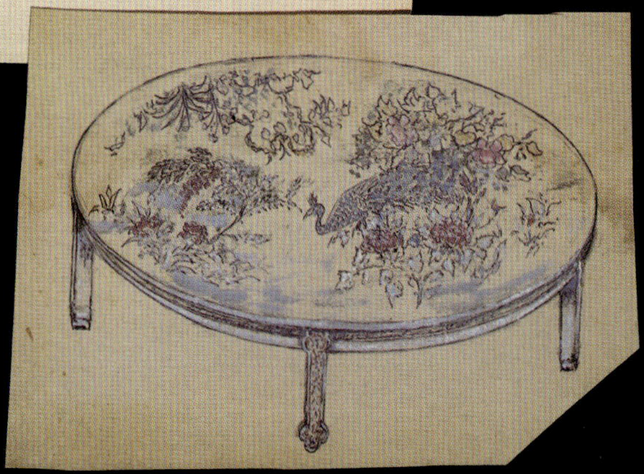

23
Preparatory study for a folding screen
Colored pencil on board
10¼ × 11¼ inches
Collection of Mr. and
Mrs. Richard Kuehne

24
Preparatory study for a folding screen
Colored pencil on paper
13⅛ × 10¾ inches
Collection of Mr. and
Mrs. Richard Kuehne

25
Preparatory study for a round table,
peacock design
Colored pencil on paper
8 × 11¼ inches
Collection of Mr. and
Mrs. Richard Kuehne

26
Picture frame
4¼ inches-wide cassetta-style frame, with incised corner decoration employing flower and trailing-leaf design
Silver leaf over red bole
13⅛ × 18⅛ inches sight size
Signed on verso in pencil

27
Picture frame
4¼ inches-wide cassetta-style frame, with continuously incised floral and leaf design in frieze
Silver leaf over red bole
23¾ × 19¼ inches sight size

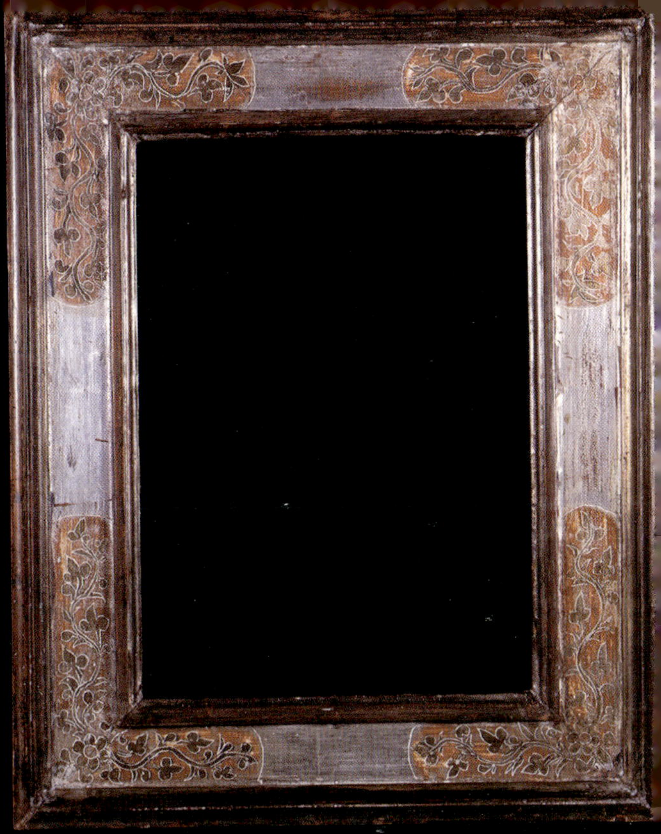

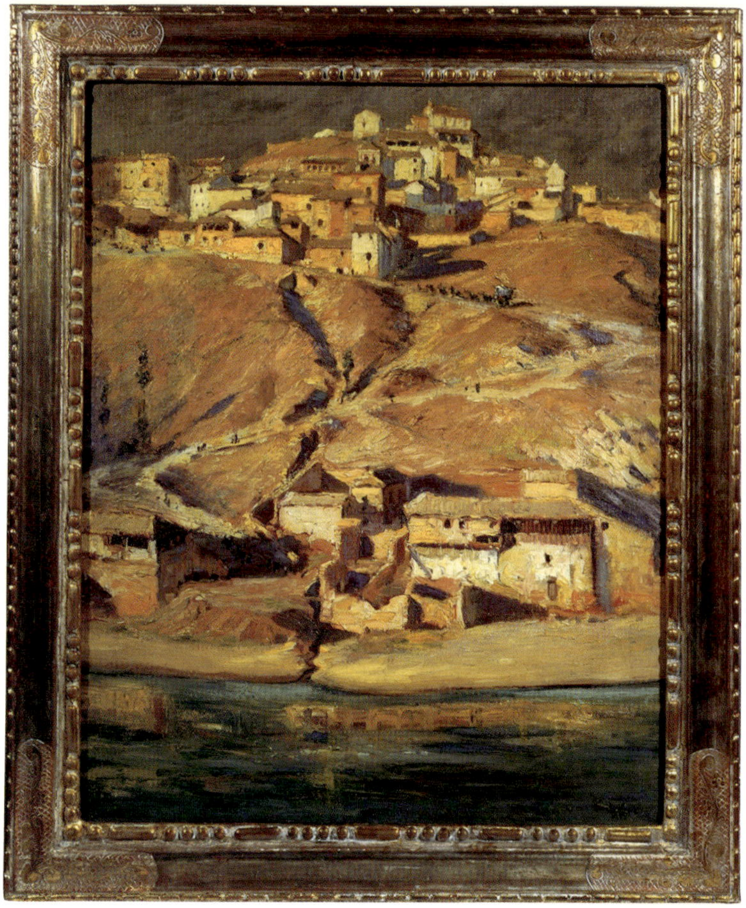

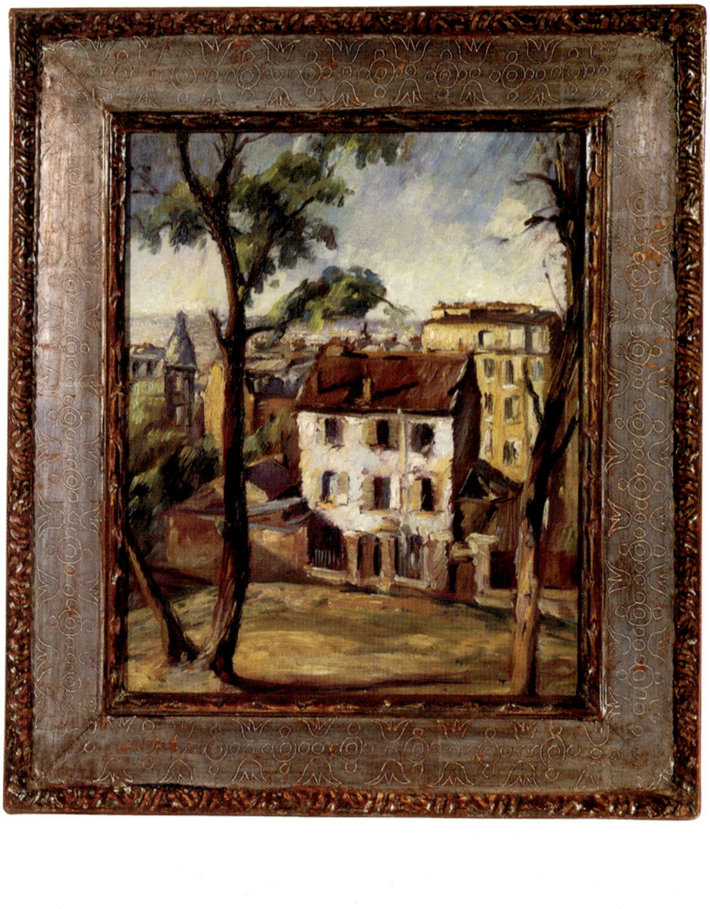

28
Spanish Town on Hillside, 1917
Oil on canvas
32 × 26 inches
Signed and dated lower right: "Max Kuehne/1917"
Frame by Richard Kuehne, signed on verso: "R. Kuehne"

29
Montmartre, 1923
Oil on wood panel
18 × 15 inches
Signed and dated lower left: "Kuehne/23"
Frame by Max Kuehne, incised on verso
lower center: "Max Kuehne"

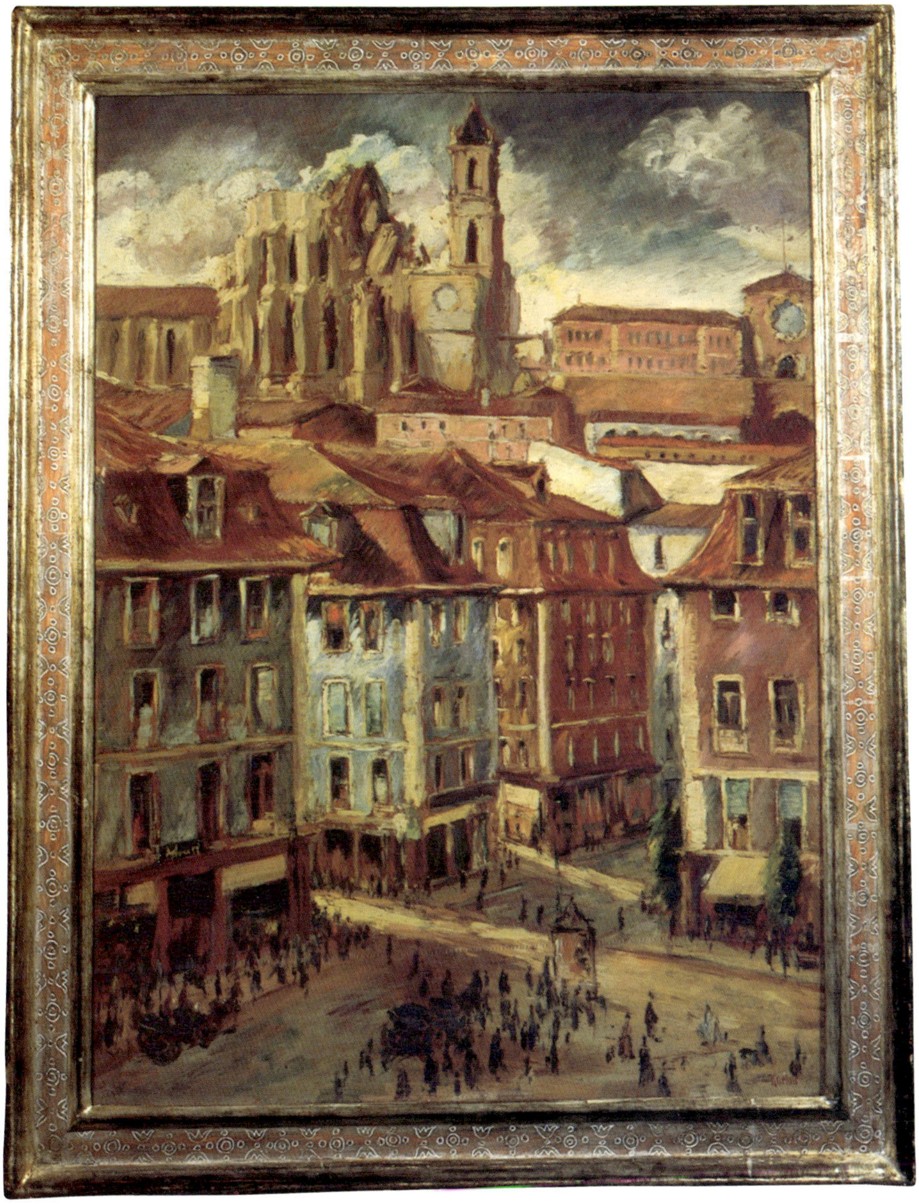

30
Plaza dom Pedro, Lisbon, Portugal, c. 1923
Oil on canvas
40 × 30 inches
Signed lower right: "Kuehne"
Frame by Max Kuehne, incised on verso lower center: "Max Kuehne"

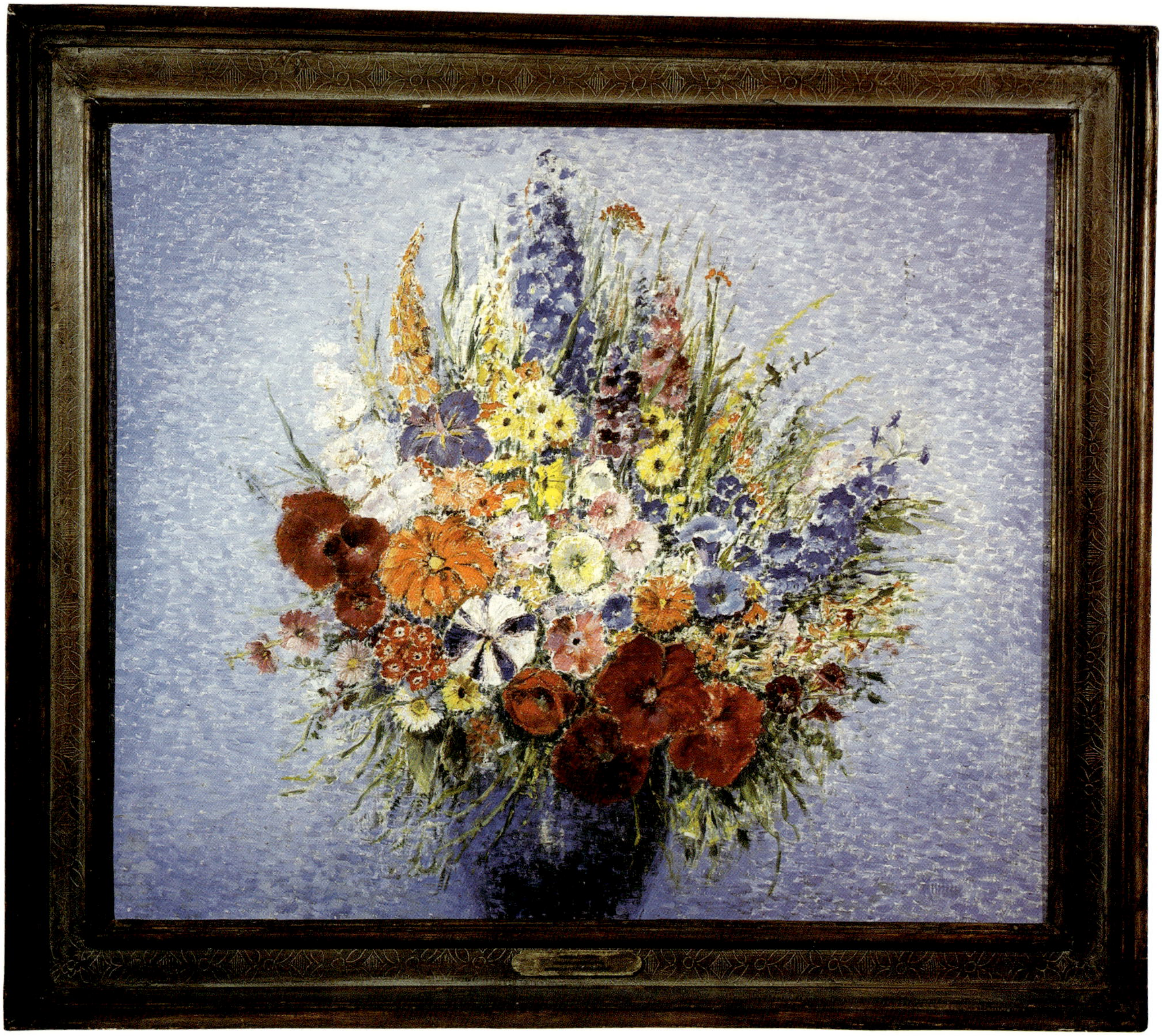

31

Summer Flowers, c. 1960s

Oil on panel

27 × 33⅛ inches

Signed lower right: "Kuehne"

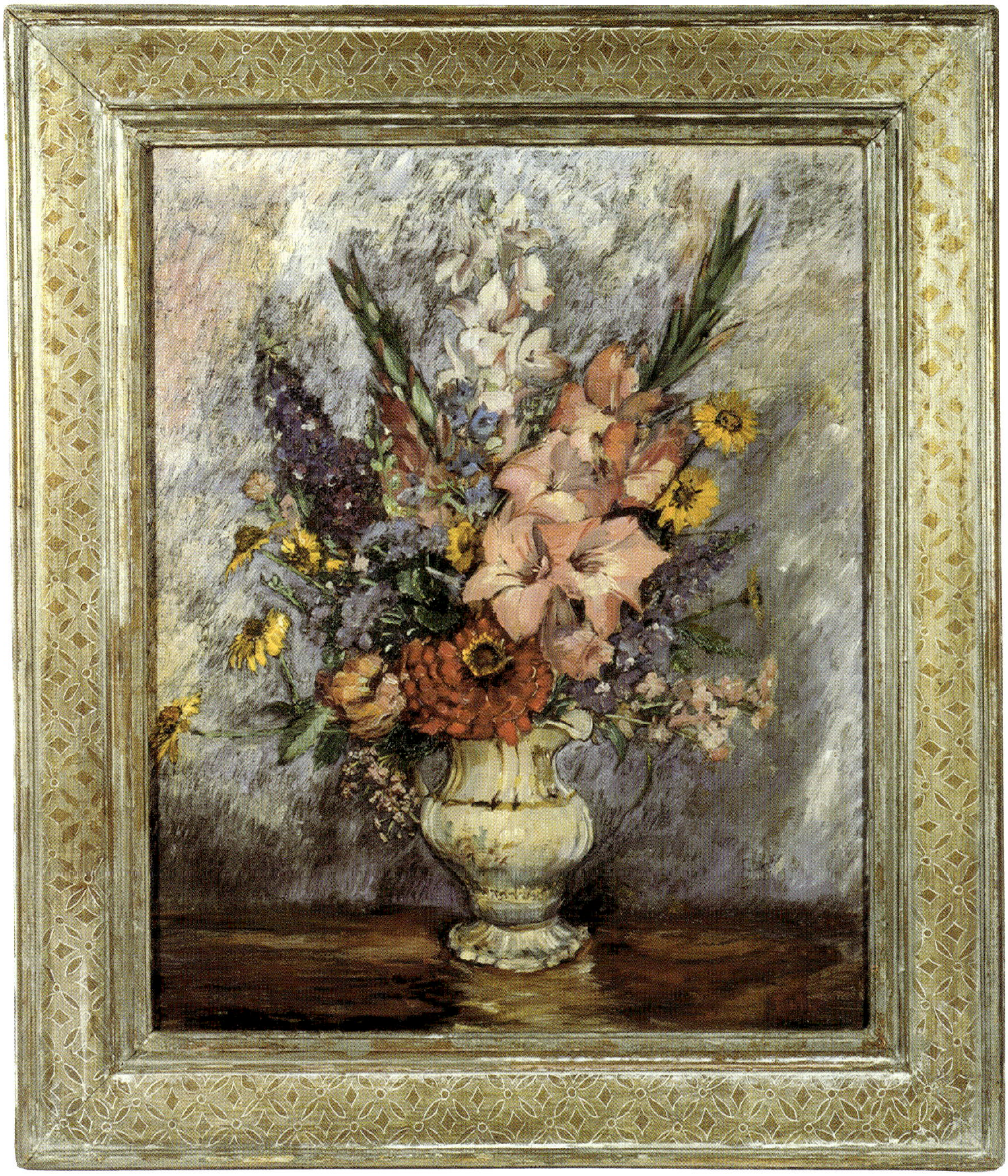

32
Floral Still Life, c. 1940s
Oil on canvas
20 × 24 inches
Signed lower right: "Kuehne"

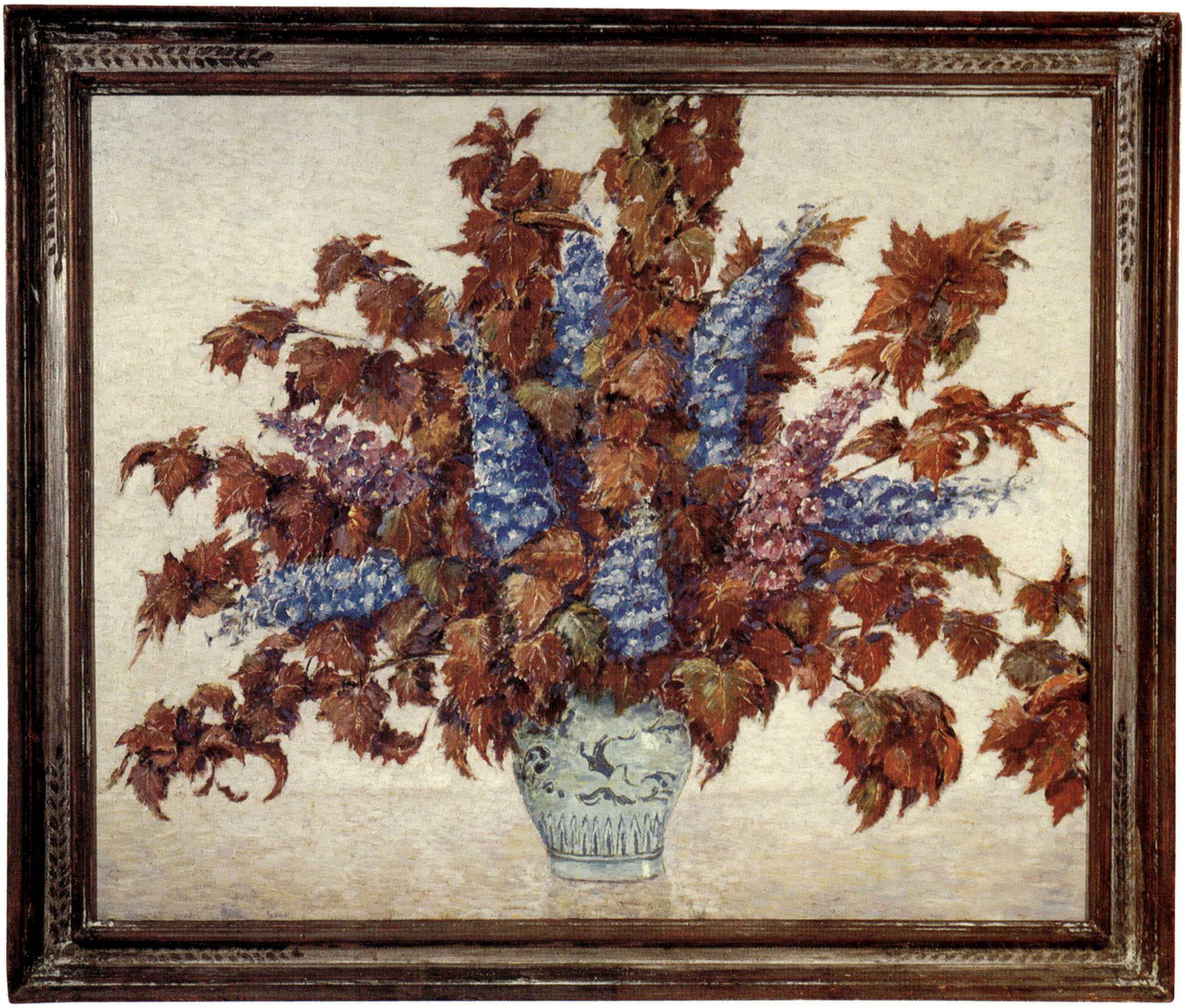

33
An Autumn Bouquet, c. 1940s
Oil on masonite
30 × 38 inches

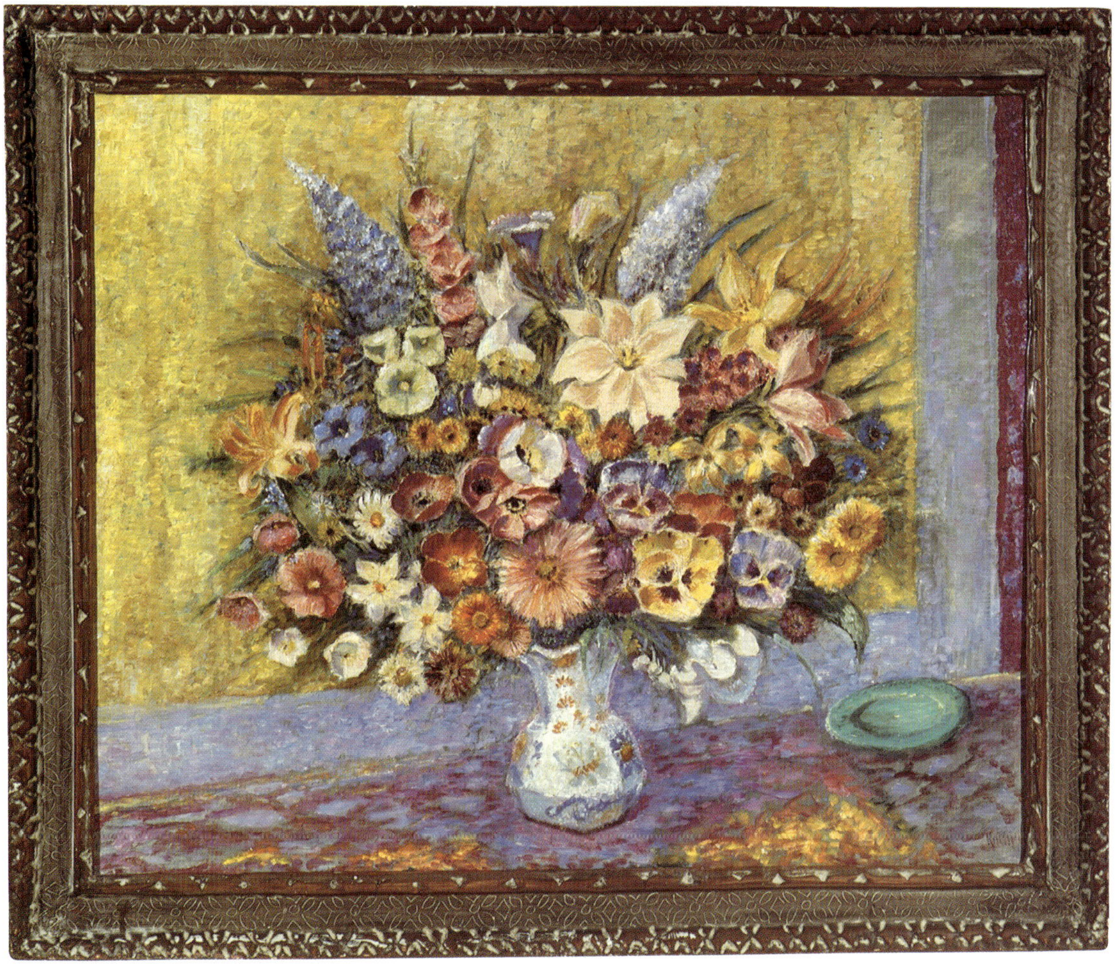

34
Still Life of Flowers, c. 1950s
Oil on masonite
26 × 32 inches
Signed lower right: "Kuehne"
Frame by Max Kuehne, signed on verso
upper left in monogram: "MK"

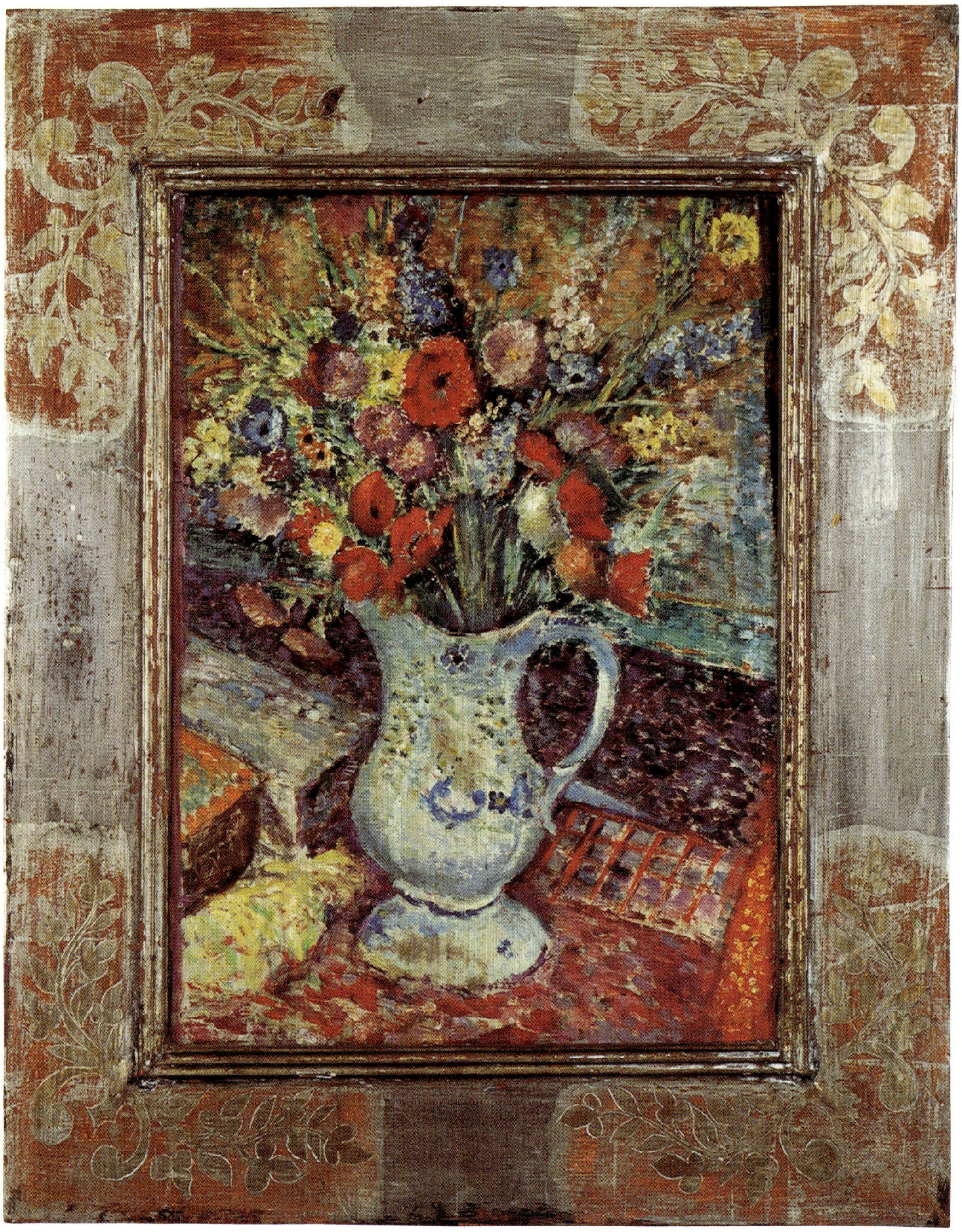

35
Flowers in White Pitcher, c. 1960
Oil on masonite
18¾ × 13⅞ inches
Frame by Max Kuehne
Collection of Mr. and Mrs. Richard Kuehne

BOLE — a fine-grained clay substance used during the gilding process. The bole is applied in liquid form over the gesso layer. Its color (yellow, red, white, brown, black, or blue) will affect the tone of the metal laid on top of it.

CASSETTA — box-frame style, dating from the Italian Renaissance. The word *cassetta* literally means "little box" in Italian, and refers to the molding profile, which features a predominant flat section flanked by a raised back edge and sight edge.

COMPOSITION — a casting material made from whiting, hide, glue, resin, and linseed oil. Pressed into carved boxwood molds, it is then removed and applied to the wood substrate.

GESSO — a liquid mixture of chalk, hide, glue, and water.

GILDING — *Water gilding*—a mixture of alcohol, water, and hide glue is applied to the bole layer. This forms an adhesive that will hold the gold leaf laid onto the bole. When dry, the frame can be burnished.
Oil gilding—an oil-based size is applied to the bole, to which the gilding is added. Oil gilding cannot be burnished.

HAZZLE — zigzag pattern incised into the gesso.

MOLDING — the shaped profile or outline of the frame.

SGRAFFITO — a decoration made from carefully scribing a painted surface to reveal the gilding underneath.

SIGHT EDGE — the innermost section of the frame bordering the artwork.

SIZE — an adhesive used in gilding, often made from animal-hide glue.

CHRONOLOGY

The chronology contains much information gleaned from two account books kept by the artist. From these account books, we are able to learn at what times Kuehne produced particular forms of work and who his patrons were. We are grateful to the artist's son, Richard Kuehne, for making this material available to us.

1880 November 7, born in Halle, Saxony, Germany.

1890s Immigrates with his family to America, settling first in Flushing, New York, and later in Weehawken, New Jersey. Works as an assistant in a dental laboratory, a patent law clerk, and a printer's apprentice.

1907 Studies with William Merritt Chase and Kenneth Hayes Miller at Chase's New York School of Art.

1908 Enrolls in January at the National Academy of Design.

1909 Attends Robert Henri's night school.

1910 Bicycles across Europe with an artist named Tompkins, visiting England, France, Belgium, Holland, and Germany. Meets his future wife, Margaret Gresser, in Frickenhausen-am-Main, Germany.

1911 Returns to New York.

1912 Spends his first summer in Gloucester, Massachusetts. Exhibits *Gloucester Harbor* in the National Academy of Design's Winter Exhibition. Exhibits at Daniel Gallery, New York, and Korner & Wood Gallery, Cleveland.

1913 May 21, marries Margaret Gresser in London; honeymoons in Cornwall, England. Exhibits *Gloucester Harbor* in the Carnegie Institute's "International Exhibition of Paintings." Exhibits *St. Ives* in the National Academy of Design's Winter Exhibition. Exhibits other paintings at Daniel Gallery and Montross Gallery, New York.

1914 Moves to Spain where he remains until 1917. Daniel Gallery hosts exhibition "London and New York Views by Kuehne."

1917 Joined by Ernest Lawson and his family in Segovia, Spain. After returning to the United States, Kuehne rents an apartment on Bank Street in Greenwich Village. Spring, first recorded sales of furniture built and decorated by Kuehne: a credenza, a cabinet, and a commode (the name of the patron(s) for whom these pieces were made is unclear). December, included in exhibition of contemporary landscapes at the Whitney Studio Club, a New York gallery presided over by Gertrude Vanderbilt Whitney (Mrs. Harry Payne Whitney). Makes picture frames for artists Edward Manigault, Ernest Lawson, and Kenneth Hayes Miller and art dealer Charles Daniel.

1917–22 Makes more than 80 picture frames for Gertrude Vanderbilt Whitney.

1918 June 26, son, Richard, is born. Spends summer in Gloucester, Massachusetts. Exhibits at Montross Gallery. Participates in the "Indigenous Exhibition" at the Whitney Studio Club. Exhibits *Gloucester Harbor* in a second group exhibition at the Whitney Studio Club. Two bookcases made for Juliana Force, manager of the Whitney Studio Club. Picture frames made for Mrs. J. W. Converse.

1918–19 Picture frames made for Juliana Force and for painter Leon Kroll. Through the 1930s, Kuehne sold many frames to Juliana Force. It may be presumed that a good number of these were intended for use in the Whitney Studio Club and its successor, the Whitney Museum of American Art (founded in 1930).

1919 Spends summer in Bar Harbor, Maine. Jessup Memorial Gallery in Bar Harbor exhibits twenty-five Kuehne paintings. Represented in exhibition of American paintings at the Musée de Luxembourg, Paris. Makes chest for Dr. Albert C. Barnes of Merion, Pennsylvania.

1919–25 Supplies frames of various sizes to artist Rockwell Kent.

1920 Spends summer in Spain. Exhibits at Kingore Gallery, New York. Included in Twelfth Annual International Art Exhibition in Venice.

1920–22 Supplies picture frames of various sizes to Dr. Albert Barnes.

1921 Spends summer in Maine. Exhibits Spanish paintings at Kraushaar Gallery, New York. Armoire made by Kuehne included in exhibition organized by the Architectural League of New York and mounted at The Metropolitan Museum of Art. Makes frames for painter Nan Watson.

1922 Spends summer in Spain with William Potter. Exhibits with William Glackens at the Whitney Studio Club. A decorative panel, a tray, and two "small paintings" made for W. K. Vanderbilt. Thirty-two Spanish paintings purchased by Archer M. Huntington for the Hispanic Society of America. Paintings and picture frames purchased by A. E. Gallatin.

1922–23 Frames, mirror, and a fire screen made for Juliana Force.

1923 Visits Balearic Islands, Lisbon, Granada, and Paris. Exhibition of Spanish paintings at Montross Gallery and Memorial Gallery, Rochester, New York. Exhibits a chest at Montross Gallery. Supplies frames to Knoedler Galleries, New York, for paintings by Monet, Renoir, and Degas.

1924 Participates in a traveling exhibition of American paintings organized by Mrs. Albert Sterner and shown at the Gallery of the Syndicat des Arts, Paris, and in London. Exhibits at Rehn Gallery, New York. Makes cigarette boxes, two trays, and panel for Gertrude Vanderbilt Whitney. Makes table, frame, book stand, and tray for Juliana Force. Makes trays and picture frames for several other patrons.

1925 Rents summer house on Bearskin Neck in Rockport, Massachusetts. Returns to Rockport every summer thereafter. Exhibits at Ferargil Gallery, Kraushaar Gallery, Montross Gallery, and Whitney Studio Club, all in New York. Makes frames for Duncan Phillips and for painters Charles Sheeler and Randall Davey. Mirror, fire screen, and frame made for Juliana Force. Bed and dresser sold to Gertrude Vanderbilt Whitney.

1926 Exhibits *Rocky Neck, Gloucester* in the Carnegie Institute's "International Exhibition of Paintings" and is awarded First Honorable Mention. Exhibits at Rehn Gallery and Montross Gallery. Article on Kuehne's furniture is published in *International Studio* magazine.

1927 Exhibits an incised panel at Rehn Gallery. Six frames made for A. E. Gallatin. Makes frames for Knoedler and Kraushaar galleries. Nine frames and two lamps made for Mrs. C. J. Blair, Paris. Mirror and a bed made for Miss Whitney.

1928 Spends summer in Rockport at Arthur Rogers's studio on Pier Avenue. Makes frames for fellow artists Gifford Beal and Charles Sheeler as well as Knoedler and Kraushaar galleries. Makes frame, table, and chair for artist Randall Davey.

1928–30 Two beds, two cabinets, a screen, and other furnishings made for Mrs. Jackson Reynolds.

1929 Spends May in Spain. *Granada, Lisbon,* and *Sepulveda* included in Carnegie Institute's "International Exhibition of Paintings." Exhibits at the Whitney Studio Club.

1930–31 Makes screen and mirror for Juliana Force. Makes picture frames for several patrons, including artist Charles Sheeler.

1931 Exhibits two etchings in the National Academy of Design's Winter Exhibition. Exhibits furniture in a private New York apartment, sponsored by the Friends of Art.

1931–38 Makes frames, tables, a cabinet, a screen, and other furnishings for Mrs. F. K. Mixter of New York.

1932 Exhibits *Main Street, Gloucester* in the Art Institute of Chicago's exhibition "A Century of Progress." Included in the Whitney Museum's "First Biennial Exhibition." Exhibits furniture and eight screens in one-man show at Arden Gallery, New York.

1933 Shows *Siesta* in the Carnegie Institute's "International Exhibition of Paintings." Included in the Whitney Museum's exhibition "Twentieth Century New York."

1934 Exhibits prints at Edith Halpert's Downtown Gallery and at the National Arts Club, both in New York. Frames of various sizes made for John James.

1935 Rents the historic Hannah Jumper house at 37 Mt. Pleasant Street, Rockport, for the summer. Included in exhibition "Docks, Bridges and Waterways" at Nicholas Roerich Museum, New York. Bookcase-secretary and a horse sculpture sold to Gertrude Vanderbilt Whitney. A door sold to Juliana Force.

1936 Exhibits *Lee Rails Awash* in the Carnegie Institute's "International Exhibition of Paintings." Subject of one-man retrospective at Kleeman Galleries, New York. Two screens sold to Arden Galleries. Two "figures," a frame, and a desk sold to Juliana Force.

1937 Buys summer residence at 29 Marmion Way, Rockport. Exhibits *Before the Wind* in the Carnegie Institute's "International Exhibition of Paintings."

1938 May, a bed and two commodes sold to Mrs. Boyer Miller and a screen sold to Mrs. [Gertrude Vanderbilt] Whitney. December, makes a picture frame and four small doors for the Sisters of St. Francis, Sylvania, Ohio, and a large commode and two small tables for Mrs. Ogden Phipps.

1939 Sells a screen to the Worcester Art Museum. January, sells three commodes to Mrs. Ogden Phipps. March, one "decoration," one horse sculpture, and one coffee table sold to Marshall Field. Applies palladium leaf to Gertrude Vanderbilt Whitney's fountain decoration, entitled *To the Morrow*, which is commissioned for the New York World's Fair.

1940 Joins the Rockport Art Association. Restores furniture and makes picture frames and furniture for various patrons, including Marshall Field. Makes screens for several patrons, including Ferargil Gallery.

1941–42 A screen, a commode, a dining table, frames, and other furnishings made for [Henry or Harry, Jr.] Farmer.

1943 Restores furniture and paintings and makes table and commode for Juliana Force.

1946 Makes screens, tables, and other furniture for various patrons, including two pianos for Marshall Field. Shortly after the end of World War II, the Kuehnes move from East 57th Street to 25½ East 61st Street, which remains the artist's New York home until the end of his life.

1950s–60s Supplies furniture to the Charles Gracie Company of New York, an interior design firm.

1953 Buys summer residence at 14 Gott Street, Rockport, former studio of artists Jonas Lie and Stanley Woodward.

1956 Wins Charles Francis Adams trophy for seamanship in the Marblehead (Massachusetts) races.

1960 Margaret Kuehne dies.

1968 March 14, Max Kuehne dies in his New York apartment.

EXHIBITION CHECKLIST

Italicized titles listed here are for descriptive and identification purposes only, and were not assigned by the artist.

As substantiating documentation from the artist's records is limited, circa dates have been assigned by Richard Kuehne, through known commissioned dates, from the artist's account books, or from vintage publications.

SCREENS AND FIRE SCREENS

Double-sided fire screen
(Flowers in Black Urn), c. 1925–35
Gessoed wood, watercolor, silver leaf, shellac
36 × 26 inches
Signed lower right: "Max Kuehne"
Private collection, Jim's Antiques Fine Art Gallery, Lambertville, N. J.
(Plate 7)

Fire screen *(Deer and Leopard in Landscape)*, c. 1930s
Gessoed wood, watercolor, silver leaf, shellac
36 × 25 × 11½ inches
Collection of Ann M. Beal
(Plate 8 and cover)

Three-paneled folding screen
(Blossoming Tree), c. 1930s–40s
Gessoed wood, watercolor, silver leaf, shellac
72½ × 49½ × ¾ inches
Incised lower left of center on right panel: "Max Kuehne"
(Plate 2)

Double-sided three-paneled folding screen
(Leaves and Grasses), c. 1930s–40s
Gessoed wood, watercolor, silver leaf, shellac
72 × 45¾ × ¾ inches
Inscribed lower right on recto: "Max Kuehne"
(Plate 6)

FRAMED SCREENS AND DECORATIVE PANELS

Framed screens may be unframed and displayed as folding screens. Likewise, a folding screen can be framed for display.

Framed decorative incised panel
(Tree of Life), late 1920s
Gessoed panel, watercolor, silver leaf
28 × 39 inches
Incised lower right: "M. Kuehne"
Private collection
(Plate 4)

Framed decorative incised panel
(Edge of the Cove), c. 1930s
Gessoed panel, watercolor, silver leaf, shellac
19¼ × 29⅛ inches
Incised lower right: "Max Kuehne"
Frame by Max Kuehne
(Plate 12)

Framed three-paneled screen
(Floral Arrangement in Pink and Silver), c. 1930s–40s
Gessoed wood, watercolor, silver leaf, shellac
83½ × 71½ × ¾ inches
Incised lower right: "Max Kuehne"
(Plate 10)

Three-paneled folding screen
(White Flowers and Foliage), c. 1940s
Gessoed wood, watercolor, silver leaf, shellac
72¾ × 43½ × ¾ inches
Incised bottom center on right panel: "Max Kuehne"
(displayed framed in exhibition)
(Plate 3)

Decorative incised panel
(Peacock and Egrets), c. 1950
Gessoed wood, watercolor, silver leaf, shellac
48 × 36 × 1 inches
Collection of Ann M. Beal
(Plate 1)

Decorative incised panel
(Peacock and Flowers), n.d.
Gessoed wood, watercolor, silver leaf, shellac
28 × 31⅞ inches
Collection of Mrs. Theodore Lerner, Maryland
(page 29, figure 8)

DECORATIVE OBJECTS

Tray *(Still Life with Flowers and Berries)*, c. 1925–28
Gessoed wood, watercolor, silver leaf, shellac
20½ × 29 × 1⅛ inches
Incised lower right: "Max Kuehne"
(Plate 5)

Decorative box, c. 1930s
Gessoed panel, watercolor, silver leaf, shellac
4 × 10 × 3 inches
Courtesy of Avis Berman
(Plate 14)

Tray *(Yellow Peonies)*, c. 1930s
Gessoed wood, watercolor, silver leaf, lacquer
13¼ × 19 × 1⅛ inches
Incised lower right: "Max Kuehne"
Courtesy of Avis Berman
(Plate 13)

Both the decorative box and tray belonged to Juliana Force's collection of Kuehne's work.

SCULPTURES

(Horse), c. 1930
Gessoed wood and palladium leaf on black marble base
17¼ × 12½ × 4 inches
Collection of Mr. and Mrs. Richard Kuehne
(Plate 19)

(Pair of Giraffes), c. 1940,
restored c. 1970 by Richard Kuehne
Gessoed wood and silver leaf
35¼ × 14 inches
Signed on base: "Max/Richard Kuehne"
Collection of Mr. and Mrs. Richard Kuehne
(Plate 16)

FURNITURE

Double-bed headboard
(Long Grasses with Patterned Border), c. 1925–35
Gessoed wood, watercolor, silver leaf, shellac
48¼ × 57⅞ × 1½ inches
Incised in center: "Max Kuehne"
(not illustrated)

Chest *(Horses in a Landscape)*, c. 1930s
Four drawers lined with Chinese wallpaper, metal knobs as pulls
Gessoed wood, watercolor, silver leaf, shellac
29½ × 31 × 18¼ inches
Signed on lower bottom drawer: "Max Kuehne"
Collection of Mr. and Mrs. Richard Kuehne
(Plate 22)

Round table *(Peacock and Foliage)*, c. 1930s
Gessoed wood, watercolor, silver leaf, lacquer
15⅛ × 39¼ inches
Incised center right: "Max Kuehne"
Baker/Pisano Collection
(Plate 18)

Door with double-sided incised painting
(Bouquet of Flowers and *Barley Sheaf Farm)*, mid 1930s
Gessoed wood, watercolor, silver leaf, lacquer
78 × 30½ inches
Private collection

Commissioned by Juliana Force for her home. One side of the door depicts her country house, Barley Sheaf Farm (Holicong, Bucks County, Pennsylvania).
(page 37, figure 14)

Cocktail table *(Primroses)*, c. 1930s–40s
Gessoed wood, watercolor, silver leaf, lacquer
16½ × 42 × 18⅜ inches
Incised lower right: "Max Kuehne"
(Plate 21)

Cocktail table *(Cluster of Copper Flowers)*, c. 1940s
Gessoed wood, watercolor, silver leaf, lacquer
16½ × 41 × 18 inches
Incised lower right: "Max Kuehne"
(Plate 9)